How To Evolve Your Business With Sales, Marketing, and Customer Service

Motivation, Goals, and Decision Making:

Book 1

Jason Gansen

http://amazon.com/author/jasongansen

Copyright © 2014 Jason Gansen
All rights reserved.

ISBN-13: 978-1503387133
ISBN-10: 1503387135

DEDICATION

This book is dedicated to all my students past, present, and future. To all of my mentors, teachers, co-workers, managers, employees, clients, and prospects that helped me learn so much along the way.

Most of all, I dedicate this book to my mom, dad, and grandparents for raising me right. They taught me honesty, integrity, and work ethic. Without them, I don't know where I would be today. Thank you for teaching me that with a little hard work, motivation, and goal setting, I can do anything or be anyone I choose.

ACKNOWLEDGMENTS

I would like to thank the following people for their knowledge, contributions, and willingness to help with this book. Without your information, this book wouldn't have been possible.

> Dean Gansen: My dad, contributor, and the person who gave me my start in the business world.
>
> Ruthann Gansen-Brekke: My mom, contributor, editor, and person who has always been there and believed in me.
>
> Shauna Gansen: My wife and the one that has given me the opportunity to pursue my dream of becoming an author.
>
> Tim Morris, Ryan Thomas, Tom Wullstein, Todd Ellingson, Pam Johnson, Denny Erickson, Jamie S., Heidi at Sunny Radio, and Teresa: for providing your knowledge, information, and anecdotes for this book.

DISCLAIMER

No part of this publication may be reproduced or transmitted in any form or by any means, mechanical or electronic, including photocopying or recording, or by any information storage and retrieval system, or transmitted by email without permission in writing from the publisher or author.

The information contained in this book is meant to provide the reader with the basic knowledge and guide for the subject content. While all attempts have been made to verify the information provided in this publication, neither the author nor the publisher assumes any responsibility for errors or omissions. The publisher and author do not offer any legal or other professional advice.

You are advised to contact and consult with experts in the appropriate professions. It is your responsibility alone and not that of the author or publisher to make sure you follow all rules, applicable laws, regulations, and governances including international, federal, state and local governing professional licensing, business practices, advertising, and all other aspects of doing business in the US, Canada or any other jurisdiction, which is the sole responsibility of the purchaser or reader.

This book has not been created to be specific to any individual or organization's situation or needs. Every effort has been made to make this book as accurate as possible. However, there may be typographical and or content errors. Therefore, this book should serve only as a general guide and not as the ultimate source of subject information. This book contains information that might be dated and is intended only to educate and entertain.

The views expressed are those of the author alone, and are the opinions of the author and those that were interviewed. The reader is responsible for his or her own actions.

The author and publisher shall have no liability or responsibility to any person or entity regarding any loss or damage incurred, or alleged to have incurred, directly or indirectly, by the information contained in this book. You hereby agree to be bound by this disclaimer or you may return this book within the guarantee time period for a refund as per the refund guidelines established by the channel in which you purchased this book.

The author and publisher is hereby released of any damages, responsibilities, or liability directly or indirectly caused by the information contained in this book on behalf of the purchaser or reader of this material. Any perceived slight of any individual or organization is purely unintentional.

TABLE OF CONTENTS

Your Free Gift	9
Forward	10
Section 1: Motivation	12
Motivation, Goals, and Luck	13
Introduction To Motivation	18
Finding Your Motivation, Your Drive, Your Passion	21
Commitment Level Also Determines Motivation	31
Motivation in Management	33
Positive Versus Negative Motivation	39
An Unrealistic Goal's Effect On Motivation	50
Believe In Your Products Or Services	55
Write Down Your Rewards and Keep Them Visible	59
Math in Motivation? How It All Adds Up	64
Training and Learning: Effects On Motivation	66
How To Use Your Top Motivators	69
Your Life In Balance	73
Final Thoughts On Motivation	78
Section 2: Goals & Goal Setting	79
Luck vs. Goals	80
Why Set Goals?	81
Beginning Your Plan	82
The Goal Setting Process	88
Obstacles To Goals	94
Your Balance In Life – Goal Setting	102
What Goals Should I Have?	108
Managing Your Goals	110
Week In Review Report	113
The Power of Visualization	116
Quotes On Goals	118
Final Thought on Goals	119
Section 3: Decision Making	120

Luck Versus Decision Making 121
The For/Against Method 124
The Five Question Method 129
Creating Your Mastermind 137
Quotes On Decision Making 138
Tying It All Together 141
Do Your Due Diligence 144
About The Author – Jason Gansen 145
Works Cited 147
Additional Titles By Jason Gansen 153

Your Free Gift

As a way to say "thank you" for your purchase of this book, I'm offering a free, downloadable, workbook that compliments this book.

This free gift will allow you to print the exercises and charts from "How To Evolve Your Business…" and fill them out for yourself. This valuable free download will help you get the maximum benefits from this book.

You can download your free copy by going to the following location:

http://howtoevolveyourbusiness.com/

Forward

How am I qualified to write a book on business, sales, marketing, and customer service? I started working in my dad's shop at a very young age. I learned from my parents and grandparents by watching them conduct business, how they treated their customers, and how they interacted with their employees.

I started working on small engines doing very basic mechanic work and interacting with clients at the young age of 6. I started showing prospective clients my dad's items for sale (such as lawn mowers, snowmobiles, golf carts, parts, etc.) before I was 10 years old.

After I graduated from college, I became a flight instructor for the college. In addition to my teaching duties, I helped recruit aviation students and promote aviation by traveling around the upper Midwest speaking at high schools, air shows, and to organizations.

Since my early beginnings, I furthered my business career by earning a Bachelors of Science degree in Business Administration. I've owned a couple of my own businesses and have taught business, sales, and customer service to thousands of people.

That being said, I am the first to admit, I still don't know everything, that's why I have incorporated additional information and stories from other successful people from various industries.

Some of the theories, stories, and ideas were intentionally duplicated in this book to demonstrate how they can relate to other topics. I've tried to keep the duplication to a minimum and avoid too much repetition. With that in mind, my intent is to keep you open minded and to think outside the box.

My twenty plus years of teaching has taught me that the best learning comes from repetition. While you are reading this and recognize duplication, you are one step closer to learning this material and implementing it.

The first lesson or law of the world is to always be a student of learning. The first minute you think you know everything, is the same minute you have taught everyone around you that you know nothing.

The first step toward the success of any business is in planning. This three part series begins by dissecting motivation, goal setting, and decision making.

I hope you enjoy my book. I hope it propels you to stardom with whatever you wish to accomplish.

Section 1: Motivation

Copyright 2014 Jason Gansen All Rights Reserved.

Motivation, Goals, and Luck

What is luck? Some people have it; some people don't... or do they? Does luck have physical properties? Does luck have an aura or being? People have thought luck has brought goodness throughout the ages. But is it luck, or is it hard work and increasing your chances of success that make people successful?

Either Thomas Jefferson or Coleman Cox first said, "I'm a great believer in luck, and I find the harder I work the more I have of it." What did he mean by that? Perhaps luck doesn't exist at all. Seneca, a first-century Roman philosopher originally said a version of this quote that has been used and changed for centuries, "Luck is when preparation meets opportunity." Even though the verbiage may have changed a few times, the timeless meaning has stayed the same.

"The harder I work, the luckier I get," has been my dad's philosophy my whole life. He taught my brothers and me that nothing comes easy, but with some hard work, preparation, and looking for the right opportunities, you will make your own luck.

Perhaps we do make our own luck. If you wait for it, chances are you won't have any luck at all. Couldn't you say that the more lottery tickets you buy, the higher percentage of holding a winning ticket you have?

Doesn't the person that submits ten résumés have a better chance of finding an ideal job then someone who only submits one? How about the person that sits on the couch waiting for someone to call them because someone they know were sought after and had a company call them out of the blue for a great job opportunity?

The person on the couch would say, "You are so lucky you got that job! I can't find anything."

Successful businessmen seem to have luck, don't they? What do they do to become that lucky? Why is he or she luckier than the failing businessman? Albert E.N. Gray said, "The secret of success of every man who has ever been successful – lies in the fact that he formed the habit of doing things that failures don't like to do." I'll discuss this more in the goals section of this book.

Is the failure investigating his lack of knowledge and bettering himself or is he stagnant? Does he think outside the box or does he wait for the knowledge to fall in his lap?

People create their own luck. If you want to be lucky, work hard, and follow successful people. You need to be a student of learning and increase your odds of success by increasing your chances.

So how do you increase your luck and where do you even begin? First you need to have the proper motivation, set goals, know how to make the proper decisions, and plan. Lets start from the beginning. Before anything can move forward, you have to have something that gives you that push, or drive to get you where you want to be.

This book and the ones that follow in the series will not teach you how to work hard. I don't know if anyone can teach someone how to work hard if you didn't learn work ethic as a child. Hard work comes from within once you're an adult.

I am disappointed in society today with the work ethics that seems to surround our culture. I would like to be able to go to a fast food drive through 100% of the time and get my order filled properly.

What is really happening there? Take the order; fill the order correctly with the ordered food, napkins, straws, and condiments. Does the person ordering

> On his secret to success:
>
> "Always work as hard as you can, as efficiently as you can, as effectively as you can, as long as you can. Every job I ever did, I always had the mindset that it was part of a job interview whether it was or not. You never know who might be watching you work and what opportunities will cross your path. If you are always the person out-working and out-smarting the people surrounding you, you will be much easier to spot... For me, the results have been extraordinary."
>
> -Anonymous Salesman

have bad luck when their order isn't filled correctly? Maybe the owner of the establishment or manager has bad luck?

It's called work ethic. Take pride in your work, after all, isn't your employer the one paying *your* bills? Ultimately, isn't the *customer* the one paying your bills?

Whatever it is you do, take pride in your work because if your customers don't come back, *you* won't be needed any more.

> "My dad always told me if you work for someone, work FOR them. Don't go behind their back, or bad mouth them or not do your job. You work for that person and you should work like it was your own business.
>
> I have always strived to be an excellent employee. I do what is asked of me, I offer advice if I know of a better way and I make sure that the job I am doing is top of the line. I am meticulous and highly organized. This motivates me.
>
> Some people are motivated to own their own business. I am motivated to show my boss that they can be happy they hired me. I do the best job I can and try to go above and beyond. I anticipate what they need and surprise them by having it done before they ask.
>
> Recently a person I support told my supervisor that I was the best support she had ever had in the 8 years she worked in her role. She said I was responsive to her requests, timely in getting things done and clearly communicates when I will be gone. This is what motivates me! Now I work even harder every day to maker her even happier than she already is. It also tells me that her previous support did not do these things. Not everyone cares about the job they do. I am motivated every day to get to work and get my tasks done so the 9 people I support are happy they have me."
>
> -Ruthann Gansen-Brekke

Love what you do, no matter how big or small your job may seem to you at the time. Work hard and take pride in what you do. It could mean the difference of being fired, laid off, or becoming the manager some day. It also could mean the difference of a good or a bad reference from your current employer for the job you really want at another company.

Dean Gansen, owner of Gansen Auto & RV, has always worked hard no matter what he was doing. He took his meager beginnings and turned it around by being aware of his surroundings, capitalizing on opportunities others missed, and a lot of hard work. He is now a successful businessman.

One of my favorite quotes from my dad and his personal philosophy is, "If you work hard, you can play hard." When I was a kid we worked hard, but we always took time to play hard once the job was done. In fact, decades later, we still work first, do the job correctly, then go out and have a blast.

There is nothing more satisfying than celebrating a job well done. Work hard, take pride in your work, always be a student, and look for opportunities.

The "How to Evolve Your Business..." series will teach you what things you can do to better utilize your time. You will learn how to find your driving force to succeed and prepare yourself so when opportunity does come knocking, you will be doing the things that give you the biggest bang for your buck.

You will learn how to find customers, sales techniques, how to take care of your customers so they keep coming back, and a whole lot more. If you want to be successful in sales, your job, as a business owner, or just be a better person, keep reading.

Before anything can happen in life, you need a reason to do it. Do you want to do *it* or do you need to? It doesn't matter; you still need a driving force. Your driving force is where our journey together will begin: Motivation.

Once you have figured out *why* you are doing something, you need *what* you are doing. I will call this: Goals.

After you have figured out the why and the what, we will begin your journey towards the *how*. I will call this: Planning and Decision Making.

There you have it: a laid out plan ripe for the taking. Are you up for the challenge? Are you ready to see how far you can really go in life? This is exciting stuff! Some of this isn't revolutionary. It has been around for a while, but it is great information and mandatory for success.

I have broken this information down into simple terms anyone should be able to understand. I am excited to see where this knowledge could take you, so lets begin.

Motivation, Goals, and Luck Recap

1. Hard work produces more success than waiting around for it.
2. Learn to look for opportunities.
3. Increase your chances of success by not placing all your "eggs" in one basket, but many "eggs" in many baskets.
4. Take pride in your work and have a good work ethic.
5. Reward yourself for a job well done.
6. Where to start: Motivation, Goals, Planning and Decision Making

Additional Resources & Links

1. http://gansenautoandrv.com
2. Coleman Cox "Listen To This"
    a. http://babel.hathitrust.org/cgi/pt?id=mdp.39076005053058;view=1up;seq=5
3. Insightoftheday by Bob Proctor
    a. http://www.insightoftheday.com/The%20Common%20Denominator%20of%20Success.pdf
4. Coleman Cox – The Harder I work... http://quoteinvestigator.com/2012/07/21/luck-hard-work/

Introduction To Motivation

Motivation - where it all begins. Take a deep breath, smells like roses, doesn't it? Maybe not, I suppose. I have seen more people fail from the lack of motivation or having the wrong motivation than any other reason.

If you don't have drive, a burning passion, a reason to get up in the morning, you might as well stay in bed. That is where you are headed – unemployment and sleeping in.

I worked at a credit card call center for a year and a half. The earning potential was good and the benefits were amazing. I had decent hours, a great manager, a team and company I loved, but I had lost the original thing that made me successful in the beginning of my employment there: *motivation*.

> "It is easy to abuse your freedom of schedule if you are self-employed. Even if you don't have appointments lined up, you still need to show up. Be disciplined by coming and going to work at the same time every day. Work like you are working for someone else, or you will be."
>
> -Anonymous Insurance Agent

The first six months I excelled at what I did, I enjoyed learning my new profession, and I had a descent hourly wage plus commissions. I had a strong will and motivation to become a trainer for the company, but had to start on the ground floor to learn about the company and the job I would be teaching.

Then a strange thing happened. I learned there was really no chance of becoming a trainer in the next several years, if at all. I had excelled to the top of my team in sales and learned the ins and outs fairly quickly.

Over the next six months I became stagnant. The work became mind numbing and didn't let me grow. The basics of the job was to give people their balances, take payments, settle transaction disputes, then sell them something, day in and day out. I took around 60 to 100 calls a day with several clients being upset about their situation. Clients swore at me and chewed me out for nothing I did or had control over.

I stopped growing; I didn't get the chance to move into management or the training job I was led to believe I would get. I wasn't utilizing my education or experience. I lost my motivation and belief in myself.

My sales dropped. I hated talking to the customers on the phone and I took voluntary time off without pay any time the phones were slow. It got to the point where my paycheck would barely pay for my awesome benefits because I left early every day.

Here I was - an educated man, successful in the past, had done great things, and I was failing miserably in a downward spiral. I hated my job so much that I would literally be in tears on the way to work some mornings.

What happened to me? I knew I could do the job because I had done it for six months and had been really successful at it. My manager even had me mentor others on the team who were struggling.

I was a thirty-something man that had been a pilot, captain, instructor, business owner, public speaker, and motivator and I was crying on the way to work and couldn't pay my bills. I LOST MY MOTIVATION!

So how important is motivation? It is really everything. Without it, anything you do is going to be nearly impossible.

I will return to my story a little later to let you know what else happened. Then we will examine what I did, and what I could have done as an alternative.

But first, allow me to introduce you to Dr. Tom Wullstein, PharmD and owner of Brandon Healthmart. http://www.brandonhealthmart.com He is a doctor of pharmacology and responsible for all areas of his business.

Tom started working as a pharmacist for another company right out of college. He had job security; he didn't have to worry about marketing, funding the business, payroll, or a lot of other things his boss did. So, why would Tom want to go from little responsibility (comparatively), decent pay, and security to the worries of a small business owner? He was motivated.

Tom told me he was extremely good at his job. He didn't tell me that in a conceded way, but as a matter-of-fact. I've been his client for a couple years now, so I know this to be true.

Tom said he was very busy filling prescriptions and helping the owners to be successful. Since he was very good at his job, he was paired up with coworkers to train them to be as good and efficient as he was. There was a huge problem though. He was paid the same as the coworkers he was training.

Eventually, he got to a point where the clients became a number as he filled more and more prescriptions. Tom also got paid the same if he filled 800 prescriptions a day or 500. He didn't care anymore about the clients as he focused more on getting the prescriptions filled and moving on to the next person. He became so distant from the people he was helping, that he didn't care if they went across the street to another pharmacy. There was always plenty to keep him busy.

One day, Tom reflected on why he wanted to be a pharmacist. He loves what he does and genuinely loves the people he was trying to help. He didn't like that he couldn't focus on the client any more. He didn't like that the person sitting next to him was making the same wages. He didn't like that he got paid the same regardless of how hard he was working. He had lost his motivation and stopped growing as a professional.

Tom said that was the drive he needed to start his own business. He re-evaluated why he was doing what he was doing and decided he needed a big change!

Tom found a new driving force. He found new motivation. He found his passion again and opened his own pharmacy. Now he can focus on the customer experience and enjoys his profession again.

Motivation Recap

1. It is difficult, or near impossible to succeed without motivation.
2. You need to find what drives you, what is your burning desire, what gets you out of bed?
3. A lack of growth or purpose is a motivation killer.
4. Losing sight of your original motivation will deteriorate your performance.
5. The proper motivation can help you do extraordinary things. Things you wouldn't think you could normally do.

Additional Resources & Links

1. http://www.brandonhealthmart.com

Finding Your Motivation, Your Drive, Your Passion

In my first example, I explained how I lost my drive at the credit card company. I also explained how Tom Wullstein found his passion and drive again by opening his own business. How can you figure out what your passion and driving force is? Where does your motivation come from?

Finding your true motivation takes a little soul searching. Finding out what really drives you can be a little tricky because it can be masked. What you think might drive you, might not be your true motivation.

The original motivation for my credit card job was the pay and benefits, but I didn't fool myself for long. When it came down to it, the thought of becoming a trainer or advancing into management really got me excited about working there.

I found that I needed growth and to feel important by helping other people. I love teaching; I always have. You might be able to think back to a time in your life where you thought you were motivated by one thing, but were unable to sink your heart into it?

I have a method to help you figure out what your life motivators are. This method will help you discover your top driving force for the major things you have done in the past. You can then apply the same or similar driving factors to the things you do in the future. For a filled out example see Figure 1.

Ask yourself the following questions to determine your "My Precious Cargo:"

1. Think of the major successes in your life.
2. What things have you done that you are proud of?
3. What awards have you won?
4. What accomplishments have you achieved?
5. What competitions have you won?
6. What degrees or diploma's do you hold?
7. What have you taken great pride in?
8. Think of any other times in your life that you were motivated to complete a task, project, or job.

My Precious Cargo:

1. _____
2. _____
3. _____
4. _____
5. _____
6. _____
7. _____

Now, write these down and place them into the blank semi trailer (Figure 2). Semis usually carry valuable merchandise, so I will call your accomplishments, My Precious Cargo.

The next step is to think about what has helped you accomplish your achievements. These are the things that carry you, your wheels, My Driving Force, otherwise known as My Abilities. Write down your driving force into the wheels, undercarriage, and gas tank of the semi tractor and trailer (Figure 2).

Ask yourself the following questions to determine your "My Driving Force:"

1. What talents do you possess?
2. What training do you have?
3. What skills have you acquired?
4. What abilities do you have?
5. What are you proficient at?
6. What types of experiences do you have?
7. What do you love to do?

My Driving Force:

1. _____

2. _____

3. _____

4. _____

5. _____

6. _____

7. _____

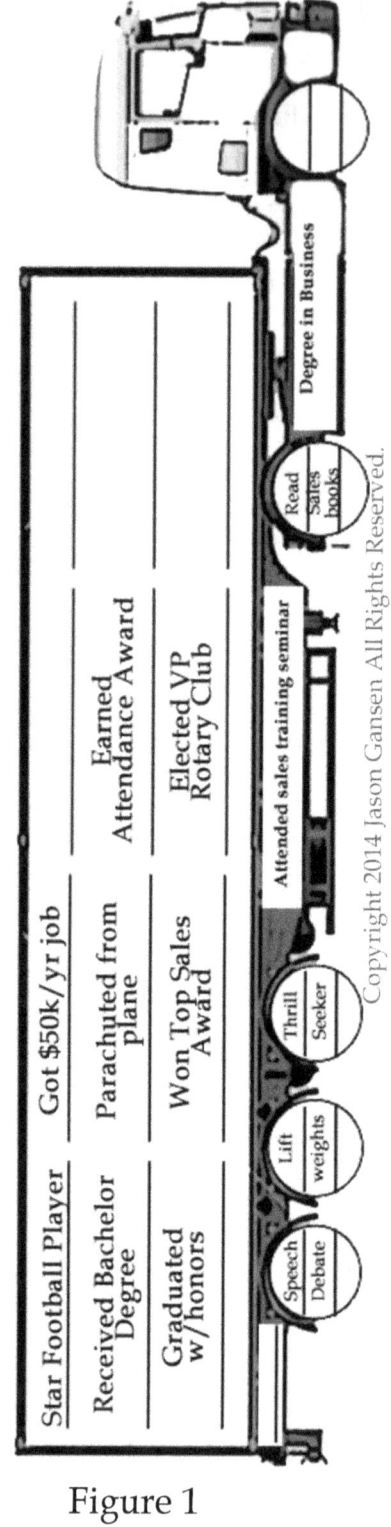

Figure 1

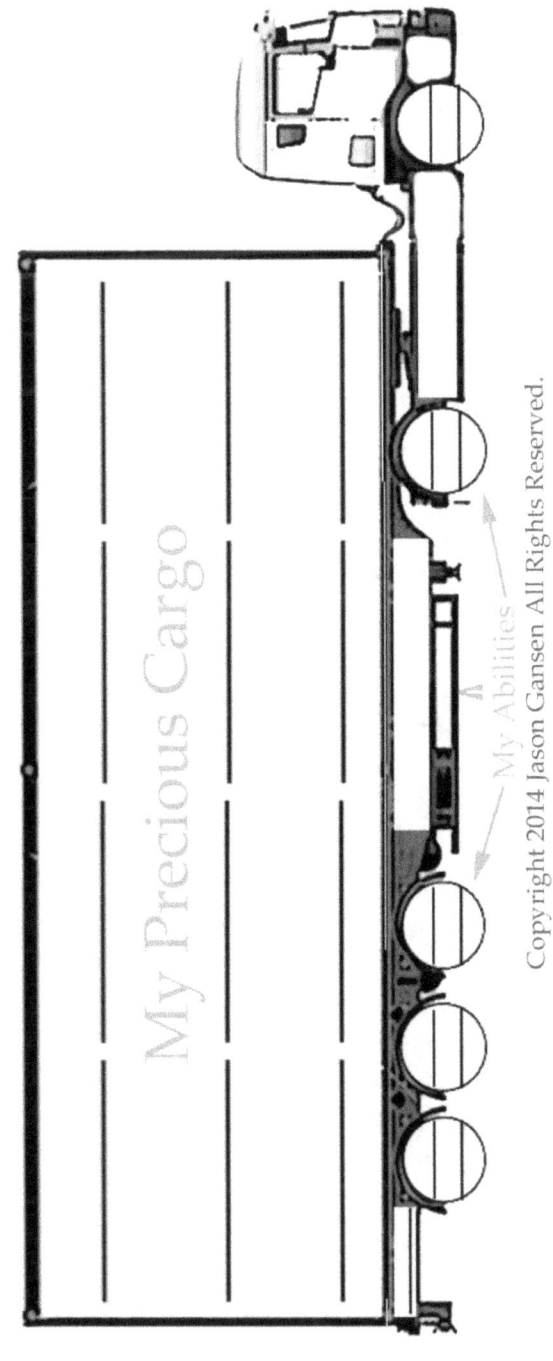

Figure 2

Now you need to examine why you were able to achieve what you have listed as My Precious Cargo. What was your motivation for your accomplishments? I have provided a few ideas for your desires listed below this paragraph. You can fill in other motivators as needed on the left column of the chart (Figure 4) or in the following list.

Desires:

1. Acceptance
2. Award(s)
3. Winning
4. Challenge
5. Connections
6. Fear
7. Fear of Loss
8. Feeling of Accomplishment
9. Freedom
10. Friendship
11. Helping Others
12. Money/Financial Gain
13. Obligation
14. Peer Pressure
15. Pleasure
16. Pleasing Others
17. Pressure
18. Pride
19. Recognition
20. Security
21. Self Satisfaction
22. Threatened

23. _____

24. _____

25. _____

After you write in any additional motivators in the left column of Figure 4, write in My Precious Cargo from your semi trailer from Figure 2 across the top row in Figure 4, one for each column.

Now follow each column and place an "X" in each motivator down the column for each of your accomplishments (My Precious Cargo). The table below (Figure 3) shows an example.

My Precious Cargo → Motivation ↓	Star Football Player	Received Bachelor Degree	Graduated w/honors	Got $50k/yr job	Parachuted from plane	Won Top Sales Award	Earned Attendance Award	Elected VP Rotary Club	Total # of "X's"
Acceptance	X							X	2
Award(s)			X			X	X		3
Winning	X		X	X		X		X	5
Challenge	X	X	X		X	X	X	X	7
Connections								X	1
Fear					X				1
Fear of Loss		X							1
Feeling of Accomplishment	X	X	X	X		X	X	X	7
Freedom		X		X					2
Friendship	X							X	2
Helping Others							X		1
Money/Financial Gain		X	X	X		X	X		5
Obligation		X					X	X	3
Peer Pressure	X	X			X			X	4
Pleasure	X				X				2
Pleasing Others	X	X					X		3
Pressure	X			X					2
Pride	X		X				X	X	4
Recognition	X		X			X	X	X	5
Security		X	X	X					3
Self Satisfaction	X	X	X		X	X			5
Threatened				X					1

Copyright 2014 Jason Gansen All Rights Reserved.

Figure 3

Motivation ↓ / My Precious Cargo →	Star Football Player	Received Bachelor Degree	Graduated w/honors	Got $50k/yr job	Parachuted from plane	Won Top Sales Award	Earned Attendance Award	Elected VP Rotary Club			Total # of "X's"
Acceptance											
Award(s)											
Winning											
Challenge											
Connections											
Fear											
Fear of Loss											
Feeling of Accomplishment											
Freedom											
Friendship											
Helping Others											
Money/Financial Gain											
Obligation											
Peer Pressure											
Pleasure											
Pleasing Others											
Pressure											
Pride											
Recognition											
Security											
Self Satisfaction											
Threatened											
Copyright 2014 Jason Gansen All Rights Reserved.											

Figure 4

Now go across each one of the motivators and count the X's to see which rows (motivators) have the most number of X's. Write down the top 5 motivators with the most number of X's. These are your top motivators.

Example 5 Top Motivators (From Figure 3)

1. Challenge
2. Feeling of Accomplishment
3. I like to win
4. Money and Financial Gain

5. Recognition

Your 5 Top Motivators

1. _____

2. _____

3. _____

4. _____

5. _____

Now you should have a pretty good idea what has motivated you in the past. The challenge comes with personal development and growth. Has your motivators changed during time? Do your past motivators still motivate you? Have you been married/divorced, had children, or have a close loved one pass away recently? Have you had any other major life changes that could affect your current motivational factors?

These are all factors you will have to consider when deciding what your current top motivators are. In fact, if you have had a major life change, maybe you could go back and figure out your top motivators again, but base it on your current life philosophies, values, morals, ethics, points of view, or other considerations that weren't a factor when you originally accomplished those goals.

My Driving Force from the semi tires, undercarriage, and gas tank are the skills that will or could help you complete future tasks. If none of these skills will help you accomplish your goals, you will need to figure out what skills are needed and who could possibly help you. We will discuss skill advancement in the chapter, "Training and Learning: Effects On Motivation." You can re-write your skills here that will help you in the future, or write down skills you need to develop.

My Driving Force – Your Skills or Areas of Development

1. _____
2. _____
3. _____
4. _____
5. _____
6. _____
7. _____
8. _____
9. _____
10. _____

Finding Your Motivation, Your Drive, Your Passion Recap

1. Look to the past for successes in your life to determine your motivators.
2. Do a little soul searching to discover new motivators.
3. Everyone has different things that drive him or her.
4. Use your "Top Motivators" as a start to help you find motivation and accomplish your future goals.
5. Your past motivators could change as you mature and after major life events occur.

Additional Resources & Links

1. http://www.howtoevolveyourbusiness.com
2. The Top 10 Employee Motivators – and Demotivators: http://www.lvb.com/article/20130715/LVB01/307119989/The-top-10-employee-motivators-%E2%80%93-and-demotivators

Commitment Level Also Determines Motivation

If you want to succeed and are inspired, you have desire. If you have persistence and don't get discouraged or distracted, you have commitment.

According to one source, to determine the lack of ability or lack of commitment, you need to ask yourself the following questions (Michener, Fleishman, & Vaske, 1976):

1. How difficult are the tasks being assigned? Is this something that I can do, or have done in the past?
2. How capable am I? I have had the proper training and knowledge or physical capabilities to perform the duties required of the task(s).
3. How hard am I trying to succeed at the job? Am I giving 100% or could I do better?
4. How much improvement am I making? As I continue and learn the task or project, am I getting better or faster?

Questions 1 and 2 determine whether or not you have the ability to perform the task(s). Questions 3 and 4 determine whether or not you have commitment.

Without commitment, you won't have enough motivation to complete the job on time or at least as adequately as you could have.

How dedicated are you to your company, products, or cause? Without commitment, your presentations to clients won't be convincing, you won't get as much accomplished, and you will ultimately lose motivation to continue.

I have an addition to my credit card story I began in the Introduction to Motivation chapter. One of the products I had to sell was a huge moneymaker for the company. The clients didn't use the product very often and it was expensive.

Since the product was very lucrative, its sales were used to measure an employee's bonuses and performance reviews. In the beginning, I was extremely good selling it. I quickly moved to the top of the team and remained there for quite awhile. I was even given a mentoring opportunity on my team to help others not as successful at selling it. I enjoyed selling it originally for the challenge and I believed I was truly helping the clients.

After dozens of calls from mad clients over several months, I learned it wasn't as beneficial to the clients as I was led to believe. I continued the successful sales of the product even though my heart wasn't in it anymore.

My sales began to slip. During a call with a client, I sold the product to someone for $250 per month. This was about ten times higher than the average. I was impressed with my sales ability, but it disgusted me to my core.

I couldn't sleep that night. I felt like I really ripped that client off. They paid a lot more than they should have for a product they probably wouldn't be able to use.

After that day, I refused to sell the product any longer. My sales in all areas plummeted. After losing hope for becoming a trainer or manager and the decimation of my sales, my commitment to the company deteriorated to the point of no return.

If you don't believe in what you are selling, you can't sell it. If you don't believe in your company, you can't excel and move up the ladder. If you don't believe in the cause you are working towards, you can't win.

Commitment is absolutely necessary to complete the motivation puzzle. For more information on commitment go to the following link:
http://ctb.ku.edu/en/table-of-contents/leadership/leadership-functions/build-sustain-commitment/main

This link will provide you with a lot of good information to help further your understanding of commitment. Here you will find the "What, When, Why, and How" of commitment.

Commitment Level Also Determines Motivation Recap

1. Determine if your motivation issue is a lack of ability or a lack of commitment.
2. How dedicated are you to your cause?
3. Do you believe in your company, products, or cause?
4. Do you believe in yourself and your ability to perform?

Additional Resources & Links

1. Building and Sustaining Commitment: http://ctb.ku.edu/en/table-of-contents/leadership/leadership-functions/build-sustain-commitment/main

Motivation in Management

Motivation in management has entire books dedicated to the subject. I won't get too in depth, but I wouldn't feel right discussing motivation without dedicating a little to this topic.

Being a manager is challenging and can be tricky at times. A manager is responsible for a whole lot of stuff. Being able to motivate a team properly can make the difference between a good manager and a great manager. It can also make the difference from being a mediocre manager and a crappy one.

The cool thing is, a manager that doesn't know the work very well can become a great manager if they can properly delegate duties and motivate their team.

I've had a couple really bad managers that became a succubus to my soul. I've also had managers that inspired me to greatness, helping me to achieve things I didn't know I was capable of.

Improper motivation is capable of transforming a person from an inspiring workaholic to a person that shows up late, misses work often, and does poor to second-rate work.

Let me give you an example from my personal experience. I had a job once where I had one of the best managers ever. A series of unfortunate events led me to have another manager with the same company that was one of the worst. The first manager pushed me and motivated me to a point of making me feel alive, needed, and successful.

My first manager constantly told the rest of the team that he was "nothing special" that it was his team that made him look good. He constantly told the other managers and employees that our company's success was because of them.

My first manager gave me freedom. He gave me projects often where he would say, "[This] is what I want accomplished by [this date]. I don't know how you are going to do it, but that's why I hired you. I know you are capable of figuring it out." That was it. I followed up with him occasionally on the progression of the projects I was working on. He trusted me and he trusted his instincts of hiring me into that position.

Wow! What a concept - a manager that didn't micro-manage, didn't act like he knew how to do it better than me, and only gave me the objective and when the project was needed.

My first manager was always there when I needed him. Unless he was talking to someone else before me, he gave me his undivided attention. He provided the same courtesy to everyone. I also knew that if I did need something, he

---

Here is the mission statement from one of the most motivational managers I've had:

"To make a positive impact on other people's lives and to help them become successful."

His point of view as a manager and sales professional was, "If you help enough people get what they need and want, you will too. You can never go wrong doing the right thing."

-Denny Erickson
Vice President
29 years experience as an insurance professional

provided me with everything he could within his power. If he didn't have the authority to get me what I needed, he convinced the person that could. That inspired me beyond belief!

I worked 80 to 90 hours a week, I worked on projects until the early morning hours, I worked on my time off, and during vacations. I completed my projects on time and was wildly successful. One of my completed projects that were rolled out to a test group was so successful that it was implemented to the entire company. My project brought in hundreds of thousands of dollars for the company.

My motivation came from my manager's praises, job security, I loved working for him, I was empowered to be able to help the company, and I didn't want to disappoint him.

> *On a side note: I had another great manager, Denny Erickson, that always told me he was proud of me, to keep up the good work, and found praise in at least one thing even if I messed up. He also made a point to tell me exactly what was done wrong and how to improve or correct the situation.*

I worked as hard for my first manager in the above paragraphs as I possibly could because I didn't want to disappoint him. I loved his praises and it kept me going, even when times where tough. It was the same effect my parents had on me when I got in trouble and they told me, "They were so disappointed [in me]." It seems like that has always been the worst punishment.

After a few unfortunate events and circumstances beyond my control, I got transferred to a different manager. My second manager constantly talked about how good he was. He talked about employees behind their back saying how bad they were. He wasn't around when he was needed and didn't focus his attention on the employee he was working with. During the middle of meetings he constantly checked his cell phone for messages and emails. He took phone calls during the middle of conversations.

I began to think, "If he talks poorly about all his employees to me, I wonder what he says about me to others?" I also began to think, "If he is answering his phone and checking messages while he is with me and I can't ever get a hold of him, what is going on?" Why wasn't he answering my communications?

I discussed my concerns with some of my teammates and they said they were thinking the same thing I was. So if he isn't helping his employees when they need it, whom is he talking to all the time? Why was he never around? Why was he acting arrogant around everyone? Why was he micromanaging his team and telling us if we didn't do "X" he could fire us? Why did our team have the lowest stats in the region?

I quickly went from being on top of my game and successful to not caring any more. I started coming in late to work, my stats dropped, and I eventually stopped coming in all together.

Negative motivation turned me into an unmotivated employee that stopped coming into work. So how important is motivation in management? It's everything!

Here is the dilemma: if you are a manager, your challenge is to determine each personality of your employees.

I am the type of person that is self-motivating and self-driven. You tell me what to do and I will figure out how to do it. I will excel and succeed. If I am micro-managed, I shut down.

There are also types of people that need to be told how to do everything. If you leave them alone, they aren't capable of performing their job. This type of employee can be hard workers and wildly successful employees with the proper motivation and help. It's your job as a manager to figure out which type of person you have working for you.

I had employees that worked hard and did great work, but if I didn't create a checklist of the steps that needed to be completed, the work would be half done when I checked in on them at completion time.

I also had employees that would get the job done perfectly or better than I expected. I've told a few people, "You did this a different way than I would have done it, but I'm glad because it turned out better than I could have done it."

It's your job to find out what personality type your employee is. Do they get caught up in the small details? Do they need to be told what and how to do something? Do they like to work on their own or as a team?

5 ways to determine an employee's work ethic, motivation, and drive:

1. Use proper questioning during the hiring process.
    a. Job interview questions with best answers: http://jobsearch.about.com/od/interviewquestionsanswers/a/top-50-job-interview-questions.htm
    b. Or you can go to your favorite search engine and type "Job interview questions" which is how I discovered the link listed here.
2. Give them a task and monitor how they perform.
3. Have them complete a personality and aptitude profile.
    a. Personality test: http://www.16personalities.com/free-personality-test
    b. Aptitude test: http://www.aptitude-test.com/
    c. Or you can go to your favorite search engine and type "personality test" or "aptitude test" to discover another test, which is how I discovered these listed here.
4. Ask them what they would do if "X" happened.
5. Tell me about a time when _____. How did you handle this?
6. How did they handle a similar project in the past?

This book's objective isn't to teach you how to interview someone or monitor someone's personality. I simply want to make sure you understand you can't motivate everyone with the same techniques.

There are multitudes of information on these topics. Go to your favorite search engine and type in any of the key words like: "How to ask the proper questions during an interview," "Personality profile quiz," "How to manage a successful team," etc. You can also do the same searches on Youtube.com for videos, or online with Amazon, Barnes & Noble, Google Books, etc for books on the topic. There are still physical libraries and bookstores that can help and your company may already have the resources you need as well.

Just remember, the only time you should ever threaten someone's job as a motivational technique is when you've given your employee sufficient chances to rectify their situation. Make sure you've coached and counseled them. Try to help them better themselves. After they are on their last warning, only then would it be acceptable to let them know you've done every thing you can and their job is on the line.

Sit your employee down privately, explain the issues and tell them you want them to succeed. You want to help them and tried to help them, but your hands are tied after this. Tell them we don't have to part as enemies, but we won't be able to continue with an employer/employee relationship after this last chance. Ask them what you can do to help them succeed.

You will never get as much motivation and performance out of someone as you would from positive reinforcement and nurturing. I've had several jobs where the manager threatened his/her team, "If you don't sell 'X' many (widgets) I will fire you." Guess what? I don't work at any of those places any more. I lost motivation and quit way before they even had the chance to fire me. I was doing pretty well at a couple of the places I've walked away from too.

And companies wonder why their attrition rate is so high? Start with your motivation techniques. If you don't and you threaten your employees with their jobs, you will be lucky if they don't come to work one day and beat you over the head with this book.

Motivation In Management Recap

1. Proper motivation can make or break a manager and their team.
2. A poor manager can turn an outstanding employee into someone that should be fired.

3. Empower your employees, let them have the reigns to see what they are capable of, and tell them when they do a good job.
4. Making your team look good and praising them will make you look good as a manager.
5. Use constructive criticism and always let your employee know what they did correctly.
6. Never talk poorly about your employees to other employees.
7. Using negative motivation, especially threats, is never appropriate for a long-term solution. Negative motivation should only be used as a last resort and with restraint.
8. 5 Ways to determine an employee's work ethic, motivation, and drive:
    a. Use proper questioning during the hiring process.
    b. Give them a task and monitor how they perform.
    c. Have them complete a personality and aptitude profile.
    d. Ask them what they would do if "X" happened.
    e. How did they handle a similar project in the past?

Additional Resources & Links

1. Job interview questions with best answers: http://jobsearch.about.com/od/interviewquestionsanswers/a/top-50-job-interview-questions.htm
2. Personality test: http://www.16personalities.com/free-personality-test
3. Aptitude test: http://www.aptitude-test.com/

Positive Versus Negative Motivation

"Are you a horse or a dog?"

One of the best movie quotes I've heard in a long time is from "Paranoia" (2013):

> *"Are you a horse or a dog? A horse is motivated by fear. He's running from the whip… A dog is motivated by hunger. He's chasing the rabbit, his next meal…"*

Are you hungry to succeed or are you trying to run away from something to obtain success and money because of fear? Are you chasing the "almighty dollar" because you are hungry for success or are you running away from bills, keeping up with the mortgage/rent, putting food on the table, etc.?

A horse doesn't really have a choice. They move forward, do their work, or get a stirrup in their side or a cane to their back. Do they work harder than a dog? Can they run faster? Are they stronger? Can they get more done than a dog? You bet!

How about the dog? Do they have to work? Do they have to chase the rabbit or does their owner provide food for them? Do dogs take naps and relax most of the day? Do they play more than a horse? Do they enjoy their belly rubbed after the hunt?

Depending on the dog and who owns them, a dog probably doesn't have to chase rabbits. I've never asked a dog, but I would guess a lot of them chase rabbits because of their DNA, an internal, primordial urge and desire they can't fight.

My guess would be, a dog chases rabbits for the thrill of the chase first and for food secondly. Dogs chasing rabbits have the luxury of chasing another rabbit if the first gets away. Does the dog really care which one he gets?

The horse doesn't have a choice. I have never seen a horse playfully pulling a plow. Horses probably don't race for the fun of it. They work hard because they have to. I guess we will never know for sure and I've never asked. My Dr. Dolittle skills are not that advanced.

We could take this further and talk about the rabbit. Why does the rabbit run away from the dog? He is running for his life! If he doesn't out run and outsmart the dog, he becomes a meal.

A dog, a horse, and a rabbit are all motivated by different things or situations. How does this relate to you?

The Dog:

1. Someone who enjoys what they do.

2. They work hard because the want to, not because they have to.
3. They seek out and try new things.
4. They play hard when the work is done and sometimes they even consider work as play.
5. They work hard for the thrill of the hunt.
6. They work hard because it is deeply engrained in their DNA. They work hard because that's the way it is and they get pleasure from it.
7. They better themselves and are always searching for new opportunities.

The Horse:

1. They typically don't like what they are doing but have to because someone is telling them what to do (society, checking account, security for the future, spouse, boss, etc.).
2. They work hard because they have to, not because they want to.
3. They are stuck doing the same old things over and over.
4. They work hard all the time unless they are resting to have more energy to go back to work again.
5. They work hard out of avoidance. They don't want something to happen, they don't want to get "whipped" (i.e. getting yelled at by the boss or your spouse, not having the security of money in the bank, or a steady job.)
6. They work hard out of fear or that's what everyone in their family has always done.
7. They don't want to try new things because of the "what ifs." They are trained for a specific job and it gives them comfort.

The Rabbit:

1. Their sole purpose in life is to hide, run, or find food.
2. They work hard because it is life or death. They have bill collectors calling, their checking account is overdrawn, they are in jeopardy of losing their home, etc.
3. They don't have time to try new things. They are too busy stuck in their situation to even think about something else.

4. They might play, but it is always uneasy. They constantly feel bad about spending money or having fun. They have to be on the look out all the time while they are trying to have fun, but life has drained them to only think about the situation they are in.
5. They work hard so they won't lose everything.
6. They think, "It's not my fault I'm a *rabbit*, I was born this way, this is what others have done in my family, I don't have a choice." It's always someone else's fault.
7. If they try something else, they think they will end up homeless or dead.

Have you figured out what you are yet? Which one works harder? Which one has more fun? Which one makes more money? Which one has the most success? Which one do you want to be?

I have been a rabbit, a horse, and a dog at least once each during my lifetime. I've always had motivation. I have always worked hard and got the job done. I've loved my job and worked extra hours for free when over-time was restricted because I wanted to and wasn't even asked by my boss to do so.

I've also been scared to find a different job. I've hated my job, but felt like I couldn't leave it. I've struggled to have money in my checking account. I've even had bill collectors call. My level of happiness and content, my checkbook, and my playtime were massively affected differently during each circumstance I was in, or put myself in.

I can tell you from personal experience that it is much better to be a "dog" than anything else. I've burned bridges, so to speak, so I couldn't look back – I had to move forward. I have gone out of my comfort zone and learned new things. The jobs I've had because I went out of my comfort zone and learned new things where the most enjoyable and rewarding things I've done in my life, i.e. becoming a pilot, teaching, public speaking, selling insurance, becoming a full time author.

What is more useful, positive or negative motivation? *They both work.* They both help you achieve the things you want. They both can make you work harder. You can earn money either way. It comes down to self-content, satisfaction, and happiness. Positive motivation almost always brings a higher morale. Greater things are usually achieved quicker and on a grander scale with positive motivation.

With that being said, some people have to have negative motivation to move forward. They need that threat of being beaten – losing their job or belongings. I have managed people with positive motivation as hard as I could until I had to explain to them we were at a crossroads, "You need to do (this or that) or we are going to have to part ways." All of a sudden, they became an amazing and motivated person!

My suggestion to you would be: If you are in management – always lead with positive motivation and use negative only after all other resources have been exhausted. If you are trying to motivate yourself – do the same thing. Look at the things you can and want to accomplish, reward yourself with things you want or want to do, and dream a little. Again, the last resort is usually, "do this or else!"

The next time you are trying to find your motivation and strive for success ask yourself, "Am I a horse or a dog? Am I acting like a rabbit?" Which one do you want to be? Which one do you think can be more successful? Which one will get you farther and can make you extremely driven: hunger or fear/positive or negative motivation?

Positive reinforcement or positive motivation for managers and individuals:

1. Contests – examples: highest number of sales for the week or month gets a $100 bill. Best stats day/week/month gets a candy bar, pop, free meal in the cafeteria, gift certificate to a restaurant, electronics, gift certificate (anywhere). I have found that sometimes if you ask, and ask enough places, at least one business in your community will give you discounted gift certificates to their business – especially if you set up a deal to buy in bulk. Sometimes just promoting how it will help the business is enough too! I've told

businesses that the gift certificate holder will probably buy more than the value of the gift certificate, may create a repeat customer, and could yield additional customers by word of mouth.
2. Create a "Wall of Fame" – place praises, client letters, awards, achievements, etc., on a designated wall with the employee's name and what they did.
3. Praise them – be sincere and tell your employees "Good job, way to go, congratulations, etc.," from time to time. Even if they did something wrong or could have done it better – let them know what they did right.
4. Play games – Any time I have taught in the past, I try to make games out of the material I am teaching.
5. Empower your employees – let them make some decisions even if it is only minor ones.
6. Use their ideas. They have hidden talent and revolutionary ideas that could be untapped. If you don't implement their ideas from time to time, stop asking. It frustrates employees to be asked for ideas then never using them.
7. Encourage personal development, reading, and learning.
8. Be genuinely interested in your employees and making them successful.
9. Help them set goals daily, weekly, monthly, annually, and 5 year. Who cares if their plans don't include you in 5 years? Encourage it and help them if that's what they want. They may just enjoy your environment so much that they will stay out of loyalty or happiness/content with job.
10. Don't micromanage unless their personality requires it. I am instantly turned off to micromanagement but thrive on my own when given a task. Some people are exactly opposite. Figure out which type of employee you are working with.
11. Ask your employees what motivates them. Have them take a motivation quiz.
12. Have friendly competitions for bragging rights, privileges, or prizes and form teams.
13. Promote team activities and a team atmosphere
14. Have team outings away from work, off the clock, and on their dime or yours.

15. Give bonuses and raises based on performance. I think the nickel an hour raise is an insult. Either don't give a raise or give them a raise that will matter if they deserve it. "I worked my butt off last year for a whole 40 cents more a day" (or a $104 a year) raise which most of it will be spent in taxes is not motivational!
16. Say thank you from time to time. After all, if it wasn't for your employees, you wouldn't have much of a business, would you?
17. Explain the "why." If people know why they have to do something and they understand it, they are more likely to get on board. At one of my call center jobs we had new policies rolled out all the time. Some of the new policies sounded completely idiotic and had several employees talking amongst themselves that they weren't going to do [the new policy]. If the company included that the new policy will increase customer satisfaction, which leads to more sales, which could lead to bigger raises or a bonus, then the policy was followed substantially better. Always try to include the WIIFM (What's In It For Me). What benefit would you or an employee get by doing something?
18. Use visualization to see the outcome in your mind. Athletes and stunt pilots use this technique constantly. Any time I have a speaking engagement that I'm really nervous about or don't want to do, I go over what I'm going to do and what I will say in my mind. Going over your actions, the resulting outcome, how great it will be when you are done with a task, or the benefits you will receive can be a really great motivator to complete a task.
19. Create a dream board – Have rewards for completing tasks or accomplishing goals and keep them visible. Dream boards are discussed in more detail in the chapter: "Write Down Your Rewards and Keep Them Visible"
20. Maintain physical and mental health – eating right, exercising, and keeping healthy will give you more energy and help your mind to stay focused.
21. Schedule more tasks than you can handle – This will force yourself to prioritize. I've noticed the more things I have to do, the more efficient I become and the more work I can get

accomplished. The busier someone is, the busier they become. If you have one thing to get done you will tend to think, "I only have this one thing to do. It won't take long so I can do it later." Procrastination sets in and your task might be done hastily, short cuts taken, or may not get done at all. If you have items 1, 2, 3, 4, and 5 to do, you force yourself to prioritize, recruit help if needed, and get started faster so you can complete everything, especially if there is a deadline.

22. Lead by example. If you want your employees to be motivated, work hard, and be goal oriented, you need to be willing to do what you expect out of your employees.
23. Treat all your employees equally. When making decisions, giving rewards, etc., make sure you are being equal. I've seen where one or two particular employees consistently get better duties, more time off, bigger raises, etc., because they where big buddies with the manager. This type of treatment may motivate that employee, but de-motivates all the others.
24. Be fair with prizes. One of the companies I worked for loved friendly competitions between employees. What eventually happened was a couple employees always won every prize while others never won. The ones that never won gave up and stopped trying because they knew they weren't going to win anyway. If you are going to hold a competition and start seeing this pattern, you must implement a one or two prize maximum win until everyone in the group (or a certain number of others) have won. If you don't do this, you will have a few that will be motivated and increase their productivity, but you will have others that decrease productivity.
25. Telling someone they can't do something or they aren't capable could motivate them beyond belief. Before I became a pilot, I had several sources tell me I could never be a pilot for a multitude of reasons. My chief flight instructor even told the class only 50% of us would graduate. I worked ten times harder than I normally could have to show everyone they were wrong about me. Not only did I graduate from the program, I graduated near the top of my class and got hired by the college as a flight instructor the day after I graduated. Telling someone they can't do something is

shaky ground. If you tell the wrong personality type they can't do something, they will believe you.

    a. Another example is when my step-dad started nursing school. The first instructor told the class, "When you fail, and you will, don't come crying to me." Only 20% of the class made it! 80% of the class where set up for failure and believed they would fail before they even started.

Negative reinforcement or negative motivation for managers and individuals:

Personally, I do not like negative motivation in an employee/employer relationship. With that said, I don't disagree with it either. In fact, it is almost required to a certain extent whether the negative motivation is directly implemented, inferred, or never mentioned. Here are some examples of negative motivation:

1. Everyone should understand if you break the law, commit a crime, don't perform your work duties, never come to work, etc. you *will* get fired. This should be common knowledge and is usually mentioned in the employee handbook, if only for legal reasons.
2. Have a written policy with consequences for absenteeism, tardiness, performance issues, or not meeting expectations with job duties, etc. For this to work properly, you need to ensure you are doing the following:
   a. The policy must be in writing for the type of offense, the expectations, and consequences.
   b. The policy must be given/available in writing, gone over with HR or a manager explaining the policy, and the consequences are discussed.
   c. I like the "three strikes and you're out" approach. After each of the three first offences, a warning is giving along with manager led private coaching if necessary.
   d. After the forth offence, the employee has consequences: Put on probation, temporary leave of absence, fired, written complaint in the permanent file, won't get the next raise or reduced raise or bonus, etc. The punishment

should fit the crime! If they are tardy three times, getting fired might be a little harsh!
- e. Use common sense and allow leniency if the situation warrants it! I had an employee that was on probation once that had their third strike. I had a meeting with him and an HR representative for both our safety so we wouldn't ever get into a "he said/she said" thing down the road. One day he didn't show up for work; a "no call/no show." I was furious! I started his paperwork for his dismissal after waiting several hours. The next day, his mom called and said he had been in a car accident and was in the hospital. OUCH! I felt horrible! Of course I tore up the paperwork. The long story short – don't fly off the handle, your employee may just have a really good explanation.
- f. Think about or discuss the consequences for not completing certain tasks or projects correctly and on time.
- g. Micromanagement – keeping close tabs on statistics. I've worked in a few call centers for a couple very large corporations. Every second was accounted for at these companies. We even had a code for bathroom breaks. Although this environment was extremely stressful, I was incredibly motivated. I knew exactly what my stats should be and what my stats where (like talk time, call resolution, customer satisfaction, hold time, etc.). I was driven to do better because I knew where I was, where I needed to be, and where others on my team stood. These companies also provided counseling and training in a group or one on one for improvement.
- h. Sometimes honesty and truth hurt, but can refocus someone's energy. When a person's ego gets in the way of performance, a good dose of reality may be just what the doctor ordered.

<u>Here are some things you should never do or at least give great consideration to before implementing:</u>

1. Micromanage - unless personality, safety, or regulations dictate.

2. Don't ever yell at your employees unless you want to degrade them, make them miserable, make them embarrassed, and want them to file a lawsuit after they quit.
3. Argue with or reprimand an employee in front of other employees. ALL reprimands should be held in private and confidentially. If you need to use the situation as an example, proceed with caution with the utmost respect and confidentiality for the person that committed the transgression.
4. Don't seek out faults in your employees so you can degrade them or make them feel inadequate. If you are looking for faults as a measure to increase productivity, as an example, do it constructively. Never reveal these faults in front of others.
5. Bully or boss your employees around. This one should be obvious, but I am still amazed from the stories I hear of bosses that still use bullying to motivate their employees. It has always disgusted me how crap seems to rise to the top more often than it should or it could be that power corrupts. Just remember, you will get a LOT further with your employees, your business, and profits if you aren't mean.
6. Not letting your employees know where they stand - no reviews, no feedback, not giving constructive criticism, no employee or operations manual, not having a job description written out. Your employees need to know exactly what is expected out of them.
7. Explain the consequences. "We need to hit this one out of the park and have it done by Friday or we could lose one of our biggest clients."

Positive Versus Negative Motivation Recap

1. Are you a dog, a horse, or a rabit? Do you enjoy what you do, do you work hard because you have to, or are you working hard because you are scared of something?
2. Positive reinforcement or positive motivation: Ideas to make work fun and enjoyable.
3. Negative reinforcement or negative motivation: Ideas to make increase motivation through negative motivation.

4. Things you shouldn't do to motivate yourself or your team.

Additional Resources & Links

1. http://smallbusiness.chron.com/use-negative-motivation-workplace-16692.html
2. http://www.2knowmyself.com/motivation/positive_negative_motivation
3. http://ifat-glassman.blogspot.com/2009/02/positive-vs-negative-motivation.html
4. http://sourcesofinsight.com/13-negative-motivation-patterns/
5. http://www.goal-setting-motivation.com/set-your-goals/negative-motivation/

An Unrealistic Goal's Effect On Motivation

I have had a few employers that thought they could motivate their employees by setting unrealistic goals. The thought behind this method is that if you set your goals really high, even if you fail, you would finish better than if you would have set your goals lower.

This could actually work. If you want to make $5,000 a month and set $5,000 as a goal, you will shoot for $5,000, right? As you get closer to your goal, some people may start to back off a little and think, "I worked hard for this and I'm almost there! Now I can take a break."

The end result is that you either don't make your goal because you backed off, or you hit your goal for the month, then you back off a little as a reward for making your goal and working so hard.

The second scenario involves setting an unrealistic goal. Let's say your best sales month ever was $4,750. A $5,000 month would be a very realistic sales goal, but what would happen if you set your monthly sales goal at $7,000 or even $10,000?

Having a lofty goal like this will definitely make you work harder, right? Maybe. There are a couple possibilities that could happen here. First, you could end the month as you always do at or below $4,750 because that is all your ability and motivation provides for.

Secondly, you could shoot for the $10,000 and end the month at $6,000. You didn't hit your goal by a long shot, but you beat your previous record. This scenario is the reason why some managers implement this technique. It does work to a certain extent; however, it could backfire, which leads me to the third point.

Lastly, the lofty, unattainable, goal could be overwhelming and you give up. Your thought could be, "I'm not going to make it anyway, so why even try."

The next section is on goals. As a little preview for you – goal setting should use the S.M.A.R.T. technique. The "R" stands for "realistic." If you don't think you can achieve your goal, you won't achieve it. A popular quote by Henry Ford states, "Whether you think you can, or you think you can't - you're right." http://www.goodreads.com/quotes/978-whether-you-think-you-can-or-you-think-you-can-t--you-re

You have to believe in the goal you are trying to attain. If you truly believe there is a possibility you could obtain that lofty goal, however ridiculous it is, you will at least do better than what you have done in the past. In fact, you may just surprise yourself and achieve the unachievable. Just remember, if you don't believe in your lofty goal, you will have destroyed your motivation.

Unrealistic goals don't just affect things in sales or business. To take a different perspective on this, lets look at my weight loss debacle. I had two months to lose thirty pounds as my goal before leaving on vacation. Of course I didn't make my goal. In fact, I barely worked out nor ate right. It felt like such a lofty goal, I gave up pretty quickly. "Ah, what's the use, I'm not going to make it anyway."

What if you had a goal of seeing all 50 states in the next 5 years? What if you want to paint your house, stain the deck, and paint inside the garage this weekend? What if you want to build a wet bar in your basement and make your own cabinets?

These goals all seem very lofty and could be restricted for different reasons. When you are trying to get motivated to travel a lot in a short time, exert a lot of energy and expense to paint a house, lose a lot of weight in a short time, or do something you've never done before like build cabinets, there are some things that need to be considered.

Motivation Killers:

1. Not enough time.
2. Not enough resources or equipment.
3. Not enough money.
4. Not having favorable genetics.
5. Not having adequate knowledge.
6. Not having enough experience.
7. Not having enough help.

Here is the good news – If you have a motivation killer blocking your goal, find out how to remove or reduce the blocker. Here are some ideas that might give you a good start. You can use these ideas and/or add your own. You can also apply these ideas to other areas of your life or business.

Not enough time - Can you start sooner? Can you extend the deadline? Can you recruit help and duplicate yourself? Can you delegate responsibilities to someone else?

Seeing all 50 states in 5 years – Only see 25 or see all 50 in 10 years. You would also have to consider the time off work and money needed to accomplish this goal.

Not enough resources or equipment - Buy the equipment you need. Rent what you need. Research how to accomplish the task easier, cheaper, more efficient, etc.

Painting the house – rent a paint sprayer and hire a couple high school or college kids or get some friends to help out.

Educate yourself. Recruit help. Find a suitable substitute.

Not enough money - Diversify and add more services/products. Start a small home based business. Get another job. Work more hours. Educate yourself to become more efficient. Reduce or re-evaluate your expectations.

Seeing all 50 states – you could reduce the number of attractions you go to in each state, eat sensible, plan your route to maximize the number of states with a minimum number of miles, buy a vehicle that gets better gas mileage, etc.

Not having favorable genetics - Work harder, more intensely, or longer. Get a trainer, tutor, instructor, etc. Eat healthy. Take nutritional supplements (at the advice of nutritionist, trainer, or physician.) Talk to a doctor to see what is medically possible and healthy.

You may never be an Adonis, competitive body builder, enter a strong man competition, have washboard abs, or whatever your dreams may be. You may not be capable of becoming a rocket scientist or brain surgeon either. Break down your goals into smaller attainable goals and work your way up. You may be surprised what you are capable of. Join a gym, go to college, pass your first class, etc.

Not having adequate knowledge - Get a mentor. Take a class. Research the Internet, library, etc. Join a group with others that have similar interests. Ask an expert or hire them to help.

Building cabinets – take a woodworking class, go to work for a cabinet manufacturer or carpenter, have a friend help that knows cabinetry, buy a book on the subject, watch Youtube videos, etc.

Not having enough experience - Recruit or hire someone that does have the proper experience. Get a mentor. Work or volunteer in the field you want the experience in. Take a class or research the field of interest.

If you want to change the alternator in your car you could hire someone to teach you how to do it. If you have a friend that has mechanic experience maybe they could help you. There is also a lot of information on the Internet, books, Youtube videos, etc.

Junkyards and parts stores will usually give you information as well.

Not having enough help - Delegate some of the responsibilities. Look for volunteers. Recruit help from other departments. Trade services from someone else. "Scratch my back, I'll scratch yours." Hire more help. Work longer hours or work faster. Extend the deadline.

If you are trying to paint the house, stain the deck, and paint the garage all in the same weekend by yourself... it aint happenin'. If you can find the additional help you need, it could be very possible to finish it in one weekend if you buy or rent additional equipment, like a paint sprayer.

All right, I admit all this stuff you've just read for the past few pages doesn't have much to do with sales or business. My intentions were to get you to think outside-of-the-box and think about how else this information could be used. Once you begin to think outside-of-the-box, you can start applying what you've learned to sales, marketing, customer service, and beyond. With unrealistic goals, you need to break down the goal so you don't lose your motivation. Remember the 3 R's: Reduce, Research, or Recruit.

Initially when you set unrealistic goals you will find that you will outperform what you normally would do. You will start out highly motivated. Over time your motivation will dwindle. Since you are never hitting your lofty, unrealistic goals, you will lose interest, start to procrastinate, or give up altogether.

An Unrealistic Goal's Effect On Motivation Recap

1. Setting your goals higher than you can achieve could motivate you to a higher standard or it could de-motivate you – it's up to you, which will happen.
2. Know what your excuses are. Are they excuses or obstacles? How can you overcome them?
3. Research the Internet, books, Youtube videos, etc. to help you out.

4. Think outside-of-the-box to come up with solutions and find motivation.
5. Break down your goals so you can increase your motivation with the 3 R's: Reduce, Research, or Recruit.

<u>Additional Resources & Links</u>

1. http://www.goodreads.com/quotes/978-whether-you-think-you-can-or-you-think-you-can-t--you-re
2. http://www.makeuseof.com/tag/5-critical-mistakes-avoid-setting-goals/
3. http://www.mindtools.com/page6.html
4. http://www.nomeatathlete.com/big-goals-easy-steps/

Believe In Your Products Or Services

What happens if you don't believe in your products, services, or company you work for? How long can you work for a company you aren't interested in? What if you don't believe in the company vision? Are you a good enough actor to make your sales presentations believable if you don't like what you do?

> "Don't aim for success if you want it; just do what you love and believe in, and it will come naturally."
>
> -David Frost

Is that just another form of the age-old question, "What's more important, money or happiness?" If you make enough money, who cares, right?

We have to pay the bills. We have to accept the job that is available to you too, especially in this day and age. We have to provide for our families and reap the benefits of having group insurance. Some people love their job, some hate it, and others are indifferent and are just there to collect a paycheck.

> "Trying to sell to someone with [or against] your own beliefs or biases or with your own personal or hidden agenda never works!"
>
> -Anonymous Insurance Agent

If you love your job and you believe in whatever you are peddling, you have an inherent inner drive. You are motivated. You probably love to go to work, work a lot of hours, and have passion for what you do. I've had jobs like this and it's the best feeling a person can have. After all, your job somewhat defines you as a person.

What happens to your motivation if you lack passion for what you do? What if you believe your products are over priced or don't work like you have to advertise? What if your company's vision goes against what you believe?

The first day of a new job is always exciting. You are motivated and look forward to your new opportunity. You get to work early and the day goes by really fast as you learn the tools you will need to prepare you for a new career.

The first several weeks or even months are challenging. You are still learning and trying to get better at what you do, but something happens. Eventually, it gets harder resist the temptation to hit the snooze button over and over. The days start to take their toll on you. Your sales might dip a little and you may even begin the search for a new job.

Sooner or later, your motivation has waned and it gets harder to sell or continue on. You may recall in the chapter, "Commitment Level Also Determines Motivation" I talked about a product that I lost faith in.

What can you do if you can't quit or you love your job but don't like a specific product or service? You have three choices – you can give up and quit anyway, you can continue on, or you can find a way to motivate yourself.

I handled my situation poorly, but it led me to where I am today. I was able to get back into aviation, as a captain, and eventually became an author. I looked for something better and found it. I was lucky.

Let's say you don't want to throw away your career and you want to make it work.

What Can You Do to Increase Your Motivation?

1. Look back at your "Top Motivators" from the "Finding Your Motivation..." chapter. What drives you toward success? Does money, recognition, self-satisfaction, etc., get you going?
2. Look at your top five motivators and figure out what you can do to focus on them and increase your drive.
   a. Money – if you are in commission sales, whether you like it or not, if you sell more of a product you don't like, you will make more money. Set a goal for the minimum of that product you will sell.
   b. Recognition – If your company has an award/reward program already, half the battle is over. If your company doesn't, take the idea to your manager to implement one. Make it a goal to get that recognition. Look at past winners, look at the trophy/plaque/ certificate/etc. and go as far as hanging a picture of it where you can see it often – like at your desk.
   c. Do a little research on how you can use your top motivator as I illustrated in the above two examples with money and recognition. You can go to the chapter, "How To Use Your Top Motivators" for additional help. You can also do a search on the Internet, ask your manager or trainer, or ask a co-worker for some ideas.
4. Take the product or service you are not fond of and get to know it better.
   a. Look at the ins and outs on everything there is to know about the product.
   b. Go through all the features and the benefits of each of those features. There has to be something. If it were completely horrible, no one would ever buy it in the first place. Remember, just because you wouldn't buy that product or service doesn't mean it wouldn't be useful to someone else.
   c. Research the pitfalls of the product or service. Is there a way to fix it or make it better? Send the information as an objective, non-biased, fact based document along with a solution(s) to your manager or up the chain of command.

d. Educate yourself on what makes you feel the way you do about it. Were you misguided in your first impressions of it?
e. If there are pitfalls, how can you turn it into a positive?
f. How have other representatives in the company handled the situation? Talk to your manager or co-workers to get another point of view or sales technique.
g. Be honest. If there are issues, let the client know about it and how to remedy any issues they might come across. Your clients will be surprised with your honesty. They will come back to you for other products or services because they trust you.

A fellow salesman, that wishes to remain anonymous, had a client that he could have helped by selling them a product, but it would have been more expensive and not as good as another company. The salesman was up front and honest about it to the potential client and told them about another company that would be better suited for them. The salesman called the other company and set up an appointment for the client while they sat in his office. He lost a sale, but ended up getting referrals from that client. The other company also sent him referrals when they had a similar situation where the salesman could help their client better. The other company even sent him a $25 gift card as a way of saying "thanks."

Believe In Your Products Or Services Recap

1. Believing in your company, products, or services provided will increase your motivation to work harder.
2. The lack of belief will kill your drive.
3. If you don't love your job, you have three choices: quit, maintain, or find a new source of motivation.
4. Learn your products or services better.

Additional Resources & Links

1. Find more quotes at:
   a. http://www.great-quotes.com/

Write Down Your Rewards and Keep Them Visible

One of the most important things I have learned along the way was to create a dream board. I originally heard about the dream board concept about twenty years ago. It has been responsible for a lot of the accomplishments I have had in my life. Without it, I would still be a really shy person that has never spoken in front of a group or gone much out of my comfort zone. It has incredible power!

Before I go into the details, I want to tell you a little about my history so you can fully appreciate how powerful of a tool a dream board really is.

When I was in elementary school, high school, and through college, I was the kid that sat in the back of the class. I did this because I was deathly afraid I would be called on. I was very shy and was careful about what I said and to whom I said it. I didn't want to look stupid or be made fun of.

I never went out of my comfort zone unless I was forced to. My favorite thing to do growing up was to have my close friends come over to my house and hang out. That way, I wouldn't have to meet anyone new, thus invoking any of my insecurities through my shyness.

During college I got a little better, but mostly hung around others in my aviation class. I was forced to take a speech class as a requirement to graduate. My first speech was a disaster! It was well written, but I almost passed out when I got in front of the class. I couldn't breath, the walls closed in around me, and I focused on all the eyes staring up at me. Needless to say, I froze. It was the first speech I had ever given in front of a group and I failed. My grade was a big fat "F."

My dream board had pictures of airplanes and other goals and dreams I was passionate about achieving. Because I had my dreams in front of me all the time at home, I focused more on my dreams than the fear I had speaking in front of people. I became quite good at giving speeches throughout the course of my speech class and ended up with a "B" by the end of the semester. Although I received a descent grade, I was still quite shy around other people.

About a year later, I started my first home-based business with a large multilevel marketing company. For the first time in my life, I went to business seminars, read books on business and selling, and listened to tapes. I learned from some of the selling greats, including Zig Ziglar.

It was during this time that I heard about a dream board for the first time. It gave me more confidence and drive to get out of my comfort zone than any other motivational technique I have ever used.

Because of my dream board, I was able to put my shyness aside and give presentations to a group of people, go door to door for the first time in my life, and meet and interact with many people I didn't know.

Since then, I have been a door-to-door salesman, I've given several speeches in front of hundreds of people, and I've taught professionally the majority of my adult life. At one point in my teaching career, I taught twenty or so classes a week to around 500 people. I've also administered conference calls to hundreds of people at a time all over the world. I was able to give speeches, meet people, and came to really enjoy it.

I've come a long way since I was that little boy sitting in the back of the class with my head down praying to God I wouldn't be called on.

A dream board is a piece of paper, a corkboard, a cardboard display, etc. that has your wants, dreams, and desires posted on it. Print off pictures from the Internet or cut pictures out of a magazine of the things you really want to have, achieve, or do if money and time wasn't an object.

Pretend like your dream board is your genie in a bottle. You have unlimited wishes for anything you could possibly desire. My first dream board was made from magazine cut outs, pictures I drew, or hand written notes of the things I wanted.

My first dream board had a picture of a credit card. I wanted one and didn't qualify for one. I had a picture of a tropical paradise, a stunt plane (because I wanted to be a stunt pilot), a multi-engine airplane I wanted to own, a house, a home theater system, a stereo and speakers for my car, in addition to many other things.

I truly believed that if money or time wasn't an object, I could have any of the things on that board. I hung my dream board right by my bed. It was the first thing I looked at in the morning when I got up and the last thing I looked at when I went to bed.

I pictured myself on the beach, sitting in my new home watching my home theater system, using my credit card, flying stunts in front of a crowd, etc. I believed it completely and I lived each thing in my mind as if it already happened.

Back then, I thought the multi-level marketing company I was in was one of the vehicles that was going to get me to where I wanted to go. I believed that in my heart as well. The important thing was – I believed it to be true.

I knew what I had to do to make more money: see more people and tell them about my company and products. Sometimes I drove around the block ten times before I pulled over and rang the doorbell, but I did it. When I felt like going home and forgetting the whole thing, I would imagine myself sitting in the cockpit of my new twin or watching a movie in my new home. I told myself, "It will happen if I try. If I don't try, it will never be anything more than just a dream."

I was forced out of my comfort zone and did things I would have never done. I talked to so many people; it eventually became natural for me. I overcame my fear of speaking in front of people and going door to door.

I have since received almost every dream on my dream board. I've had many-a-credit card, I have performed stunts in an airplane and flown at an air show (not as a stunt pilot though). I didn't own a twin-engine airplane, but I flew one every day for many years as a career. I've owned several homes, I've had a couple different home theater systems, and I've gone on many vacations to Mexico, Bahamas, Jamaica, Grand Cayman, etc.

The book and the movies "The Secret" explain exactly how this concept works and why it works. Back then, I didn't understand it or really understand how it works, but it did work. I overcame the debilitating fears that held me back from achieving the things I desired the most.

I highly recommend watching "The Secret" and "The Secret 2" and reading the book, "The Secret" by Rhonda Byrne. Some of the stuff in there may sound a little hokey, but it works.

Because I intensely focused on my dreams, and I believed them to be true, my subconscious mind worked out all the details on how to achieve them.

Creating and Using Your Own Dream Board:

1. Write down a list of your most desired dreams, wants, and desires if money and time weren't an object.
2. Print and/or cut out pictures in magazines or the Internet, draw a picture of your dreams, or write them down on a strip of paper.
3. Tape, glue, or thumbtack your pictures to a corkboard, piece of paper, construction paper, cardboard display, etc.
4. Hang up your dream board where you need your motivation or somewhere you will look often – i.e. in your car, by the phone, at your desk, by your bed, by the mirror, in the kitchen, etc.
5. Look at your dream board often.
6. Imagine yourself living your dreams, driving your new boat or car, living in your dream home, sitting on the beach, etc. Believe it like it has already happened and visualize yourself in the moment. It has already happened.
7. Any time you need motivation, think about how awesome it is to have or do the things on your dream board.
8. Don't get discouraged. Keep following the steps of visualizing and dreaming. You may not achieve the results you want with what you are currently doing, but it could

lead you to a situation that could provide your desired outcome. I found the courage to go out of my comfort zone, which eventually took me down a path that helped me realize my dreams.

Another thing you could do that may not be as effective as creating a dream board is to keep track of your rewards by writing them down.

I will discuss goals more in the Goals and Goal Setting section, but I always accompany my goals with the reward associated with it.

If I have a goal of losing 10 pounds, I might include "Going to a pizza buffet" as my reward since it is my favorite thing to do. If I have a sales goal of $5,000 in commission for the month, I might include, "going to a movie" or "taking a weekend vacation" as my reward.

You need to make this reward something that is easily attainable and affordable for you opposed to the "money and time is no object" principle of the dream board. Similarly, you need to keep this reward in a place you will look at frequently, like your day planner or hanging up at your desk. You also need to visualize your reward like you have already achieved it and think about how it will feel, what you will see, what smells you will experience, etc. Really include all of your senses that you can to make it as real for you as possible.

This method of rewards will motivate you more for short-term goals. Sometimes the dream board can seem a little overwhelming and unbelievable, which could have the opposite affect on your motivation.

Here is the secret behind visualization techniques, dream boards, and rewards for completing a goal: ACTION! If you <u>only</u> believe you will obtain your dreams, a vacation, a house, etc., if you <u>only</u> visualize it happening, or if you <u>only</u> look at your dream board every day, nothing will happen. This technique is to help you get off your duff and <u>do</u> something and think of ways to accomplish your goals. Just remember this – *inactivity is the number 1 killer of dreams!*

Write Down Your Rewards and Keep Them Visible Recap

1. Using a dream board will take your motivation to the next level.
2. Keep your wants, dreams, desires, and rewards readily visible.
3. Write down your rewards and look at them often.
4. Believe with your full heart that your rewards will be achieved.
5. Taking ACTION is the only way to achieve your success.

Additional Resources & Links

1. http://www.thesecret.tv
2. Purchase movies or books by Rhonda Byrne on Amazon.com:
   a. http://www.amazon.com/Rhonda-Byrne/e/B001ILM8OQ/ref=ntt_dp_epwbk_0
3. Search for Rhonda Byrne on Amazon.com or watch the movie on Netflix.com
4. Search for "How to create a dream board" on Google, Yahoo, Bing, or your favorite search engine.
5. http://www.wikihow.com/Make-a-Dream-Board

Math in Motivation? How It All Adds Up

The next thing you need to figure out is if the performance issue is a motivation or ability problem.

When you put all the information together, you can evaluate motivation and performance with a couple of simple math problems. If there is a lack of, or decrease in performance, you need to consider the following equations (Developing Management Skills, Whetton & Cameron, 2004, 299-300):

Performance = Ability x Motivation (Effort)

Where:

Ability = Aptitude x Training x Resources

Motivation = Desire x Commitment

Whether you are a manager, employee, in sales, or a business owner, you can utilize this information to your advantage. You can provide motivation for your team or diagnose motivation issues for yourself.

The next time you are confronted with performance issues -

Ask The Following:

1. Do I have the ability to perform the task(s)?
   a. Do I have the natural talent to perform the task(s)?
   b. Have I had the proper (and adequate) training?
   c. Have I been provided with the resources I need to complete the task(s)?
2. Do I have the motivation to perform and complete the task(s)?
   a. Do I want to complete the task(s)? Do I want to do this?
   b. Am I committed to the task? Do I believe in the company or products? Do I believe in the cause and the desired outcome?

Math in Motivation? How It All Adds Up Recap

1. **Performance = Ability x Motivation (Effort)**

   Where:

   Ability = Aptitude x Training x Resources

   Motivation = Desire x Commitment

2. Evaluate your situation based on the equations listed above.

Additional Resources & Links

1. http://www.amazon.com/Developing-Management-Skills-David-Whetten/dp/0131441426

Training and Learning: Effects On Motivation

Training, learning, and your personal skills are linked to your motivation and drive. What you know is directly tied to your ability to perform.

Remember the Semi exercise in the chapter, "Finding Your Motivation, Your Drive, Your Passion?" This is how you find your ability to complete your goals. Without the *ability*, you still can't achieve your goals.

The five key factors that can be used to conquer ability issues are the 5 "R's" (Michener, Fleishman, and Vaske).

The 5 R's

1. **Resupply** – Are the needs of the task being filled? Are the resources to complete the task available to you? If not, obtain the proper tools, equipment, or supplies.
2. **Retrain** – What training would best fit the task(s) that need to be accomplished? Once the training needs have been identified, begin the training.
3. **Refit** – Find a different job task or project if the proper supplies and training are not available or insufficient.
4. **Reassign** – Find a different task or position for yourself, or assign someone that is capable of completing the task or project.
5. **Release** – If you are not a good fit to the company and can't gain the skills required, it is time to look for a different job.

Another way to look at ability issues is by taking a look at the ability equation:

Ability = Aptitude x Training x Resources

Aptitude is your inner talents or inherent skills. Aptitude allows you to just know certain things or pick up on them quickly. I come from a long line of mechanics. I am definitely not a mechanic by trade, but I can fix just about anything from electronics, small engines, and all the way through to large machinery.

Some people are just good at certain things. Your aptitude may not come from your lineage either. You might be a fast learner or have a knack for specific skills like cooking, painting, accounting, writing, speaking in front of a group, fixing, inventing, etc.

It is possible that you haven't found what your natural talent is yet, but you will know it when you find it. Your special skill will help you achieve specific goals and could provide you with passion in an area you never dreamt possible. The only way to find it is to try new things, explore, and examine your results.

If you have found your inner talent, you will most likely excel at it, learn it quickly, enjoy it, think about it often, or be able to easily earn money from doing it.

Training doesn't always have to be instructor led. Your training can be self-directed by your own research. We live in exciting times in the world of training! Learning to do just about anything is only a click away. Through technology, we can read books, watch videos, read blogs on specific topics, find news topics, learn definitions, examine popular techniques, take a course, get a degree, learn life hacks, and a plethora of other useful stuff.

Reading is a powerful tool. You should set a goal to read 15 minutes a day, every day. If you want to get ahead in life, stay motivated, and remain marketable as a contributor to society and the rapidly changing world as we know it, you must be a student of life.

You should read, train, get a mentor, job shadow, attend seminars, get certified, take classes, get a degree(s), or watch videos to learn new things all the time. In fact, by reading this book, you are doing the right thing already! Study the things you are interested in or want to do better. There is enough information out there to keep you busy for a million life times. What you learn is completely up to you. Where you want to be in life will be achievable with the proper education.

The important thing is that you are studying and trying to improve yourself. Someone that isn't learning isn't moving forward.

I have read some really bad material and went to extremely boring seminars, but they have all been worth it. If you can learn at least <u>ONE</u> new thing that is beneficial, it was worth every second.

Resources is what you have available to help you achieve your goals. Resources can be tools, computers, devices, books, records (not the vinyl/music type), paper and pen, or basically anything that is available to help you complete a task. The questions, ideas, quotes, charts, and pictures in this book can be resources as well.

Don't forget that in addition to "things" available to help you accomplish goals, **people** are resources too. Your ability to find talent in the people around you is a valuable asset. If you don't know how to do something and don't have the time to learn, find someone that does. The capability to delegate tasks to others is invaluable.

Delegating a task can be a difficult challenge for some people. Don't be too proud to ask for help and don't always think it will be done better or easier if you just do it yourself. Use the people around you that are available to your advantage.

When you are trying to find motivation to complete your goals and find your ability, ask yourself the following questions in relation to –

What Needs to be Done:

1. What has helped me accomplish my achievements in the past?
2. What talents do I possess?
3. What training or certifications do I have?
4. What skills have I acquired?
5. What abilities do I have?
6. What am I proficient at?
7. What types of experiences have I had?
8. What resources do I have available?

9. What do I love to do?

If you don't have the knowledge or skills needed to complete the task at hand, your motivation will not be enough to carry you through to completion. In fact, your motivation will dwindle as you become frustrated.

First of all, don't get frustrated if you don't have the ability to complete your goal or task. Don't be embarrassed or too proud to admit it. If you are, it will surely lead to certain failure. Everyone has faults and inadequacies. After all, not everyone knows how to be a surgeon, a rocket scientist, and a pilot all at the same time, but you could if you had the proper training and motivation.

Training and Learning: Effects On Motivation Recap

1. What is causing your ability issues – aptitude, training, resources?
2. Aptitude is your inner talents or inherent skills.
3. Training can come from an instructor or self led.
4. Resources can come from any available source of knowledge that will help you.
5. If your ability is holding you back:
   a. Get the training you need.
   b. Utilize or discover your inner talents.
   c. Use your resources around you.
   d. Use the 5 "R's": Resupply, Retrain, Refit, Reassign, Release

Additional Resources & Links

1. Dealing with poor performance:
   http://www.mindtools.com/pages/article/newTMM_80.htm

How To Use Your Top Motivators

The entire first section of this book has been dedicated to helping you find your specific desire and help you to increase your commitment. In turn, you will know what is your driving force, your motivation.

Motivation = Desire x Commitment

Desire is what you want, plain and simple. What do you crave? What is your wish or dream? What do you aspire to be or move towards?

Here is the list of desires and some ideas to drive them to the next level –

List Of Desires

1. Acceptance – whom are you trying to be accepted by? If you want friends, be included in a group, or attain someone's approval, helping others so you can help yourself motivates you.
2. Award(s) – if you are the type of person that likes awards, investigate the different types of awards available and the requirements to achieve them. You should also take frequent trips to the trophy case or the wall of fame at your company. Visualize your name on one of the plaques.
3. Winning – are you the competitive type? Do you like winning for the sake of winning, or bragging rights? Have fun with it and throw out a challenge to others in your team or the other team.
4. Challenge – Does your desire come from completing a challenge or because the project is challenging? If a job is continually unchallenging, try to think of other ways to increase the intensity. If your tasks become monotonous, it may be time to move up or move out.
5. Connections – if you are motivated by the connections you can make or the people you meet, make sure you are putting yourself in situations where you can make beneficial connections. Depending on the type of connections you are trying to make, you can join the Chamber of Congress, a club, or a local group.
6. Fear – fear is a powerful motivator, but should be used sparingly; however, some people do work best under

pressure. Pin point exactly what fear you have and use it to your advantage.
7. Fear of Loss – similar to fear in the previous paragraph, fear of loss could keep you at a job you hate. If you need a paycheck to pay the bills and can't find another job, you might work even harder so you can keep the job you dislike. The reality of losing your home, not having food, losing your benefits, or losing your vehicle can be a powerful motivator.
8. Feeling of Accomplishment – if you are a person that enjoys a job well done, make sure you take the time to reflect on how good it will feel once the job is complete.
9. Freedom – financial freedom or freedom from having a boss, coming and going as you please, a flexible schedule, or being able to make your own decisions gives you empowerment.
10. Friendship – much like acceptance, you are in it for the friends. You will enjoy your work more if you can socialize with others or meet new people.
11. Helping Others – make sure you take the time to talk to or understand the people you are trying to help. The nicer they are, or the more difficult their situation is, the harder you will work to help them.
12. Money/Financial Gain – write down what the money will provide for you or create a dream board if the money will buy you the things you desire.
13. Obligation – you work because you have to. If you are motivated out of obligation, commit a few minutes to ponder over your commitments.
14. Peer Pressure - you are the type of person that is micromanaged or pushed by a manager or your team. Let your manager or team know that a little push or pep talk will take you a long way.
15. Pleasure – you love what you do. As an example, a ski instructor or flight instructor might love their job because during their off time they go skiing or flying. You are doing what you do because it is your hobby or passion.
16. Pleasing Others – surround yourself with people that pay you the compliments you desire and deserve. You do things out of the goodness of your heart – so look into how your work will help others or improve their lives.

17. Pressure – schedule your appointments or deadlines close together and fill your calendar.
18. Pride – you might take pride in your work, which is self-directed satisfaction. Think about how good you will feel and how proud of yourself you will be because you will do a good job. You could also be the type of person that is proud to do the work you do out of respect for the uniform – i.e. pilots, doctors, fireman, police officer, military, etc.
19. Recognition - If your company has an award/reward program already, half the battle is over. If your company doesn't, take the idea to your manager to implement one. Make it a goal to get that recognition. Look at past winners, look at the trophy/plaque/ certificate/etc. and go as far as to hang a picture of it where you can see it often – like at your desk.
20. Security – you are in it for safety. The bills get paid and it gives you a sigh of relieve. It feels good to not worry.
21. Self Satisfaction – you do it because you enjoy a job well done. Take a step back and look at your work completed when it's done. Use your visualization to remember how great it felt the next time a task is before you.
22. Threatened - you need a little or big push to get you going. I would never run several miles, but if a bear was chasing me… you get the picture. If you need someone to keep after you, let him or her know to keep on you.

The second part of motivation is commitment. Here is a list of some commitment factors that could boost your motivation –

List of Commitment Factors

1. Commitment is how dedicated you are to something. Commitment comes from obligation – like to pay the bills and provide food on the table. Whether you want to do something or not, you have to.
2. Commitment comes from promises made. If you promised to take your kids to Disney World or your wife to the Bahamas, you have to find a way to achieve the desired result or there will be consequences. Commitment can also

come from promises you've made to yourself. You can promise yourself to get healthier, eat right, stop smoking, and start exercising so you can live a longer life.
3. Commitment comes from loyalty. My manager I spoke of in one of the beginning chapters motivated me by loyalty. I wanted to be loyal to him and the company because he was loyal to me. He always looked out for my best interest and helped me achieve my goals. He helped me before helping himself. My level of commitment out of loyalty and honor toward his efforts where increased significantly.
4. Commitment comes from responsibility and duty. A soldier is committed to work long, hard hours and if necessary die for his country out of duty and honor. A soldier believes it is his or her responsibility to fight for our rights as citizens.
5. Commitment comes from faithfulness. If you love someone, are faithful, or loyal, you will be committed to work as hard as you can out of respect toward that faithfulness.

Wherever your commitment comes from or your desires want to take you, motivation is the key to your goals, but it is only the very beginning. Once you've learned the why, you need to take the next step: who, what, where, when, and how.

How To Use Your Top Motivators Recap

1. Find what your desires are and utilize them to increase motivation.
2. Boost your motivation further by strengthening your commitment level.

Your Life In Balance

The last factor involved with motivation is to keep your life in balance. This technique was taught to me by Denny Erickson several years ago and turned out to be more important in sales than I originally gave him credit for.

Your happiness has a direct correlation to the level of success you can achieve. If one part of your life is off balance, it can affect the other areas in your life.

Life balance involves keeping your personal life, financial security, professional career, and your physical well being in check. Your spirituality is the glue that binds it all together.

Your personal life includes your home, spouse or significant other, your children, your family and relatives, your friends, and your personal time.

Your financial security includes your bills, income, debt, savings, investments, spending habits, retirement savings, employee benefits, and any other expenditures, income, or financial resources.

Your professional career includes your education, position or title, employer, employment status, certificates or degrees earned, relationship with co-workers and manager, business or sales goals, and your career path.

Your physical well-being includes your physical and mental health; what shape you are in; diet/nutrition; exercise (type, duration, and frequency); diseases; medication.

Your spirituality includes attending worship services, charity work, reading your religious documents, scriptures, teachings, or bible, centering yourself on a spiritual level, prayer, joining religious groups, religious experiences, meditation, and relaxation. Your spirituality is anything that helps you relax, center yourself, and bring a sense of calm in your busy and hectic life. Whether you get your spirituality from religion or watching a beautiful sunset from the top of a mountain is up to you.

Each area of your life influences and affects each of the other parts directly or indirectly. A pull in one direction in the balance of life chart creates a lack in another area. When your balance of life chart is in balance, your level of happiness will be at its highest. See the figure below (Figure 5).

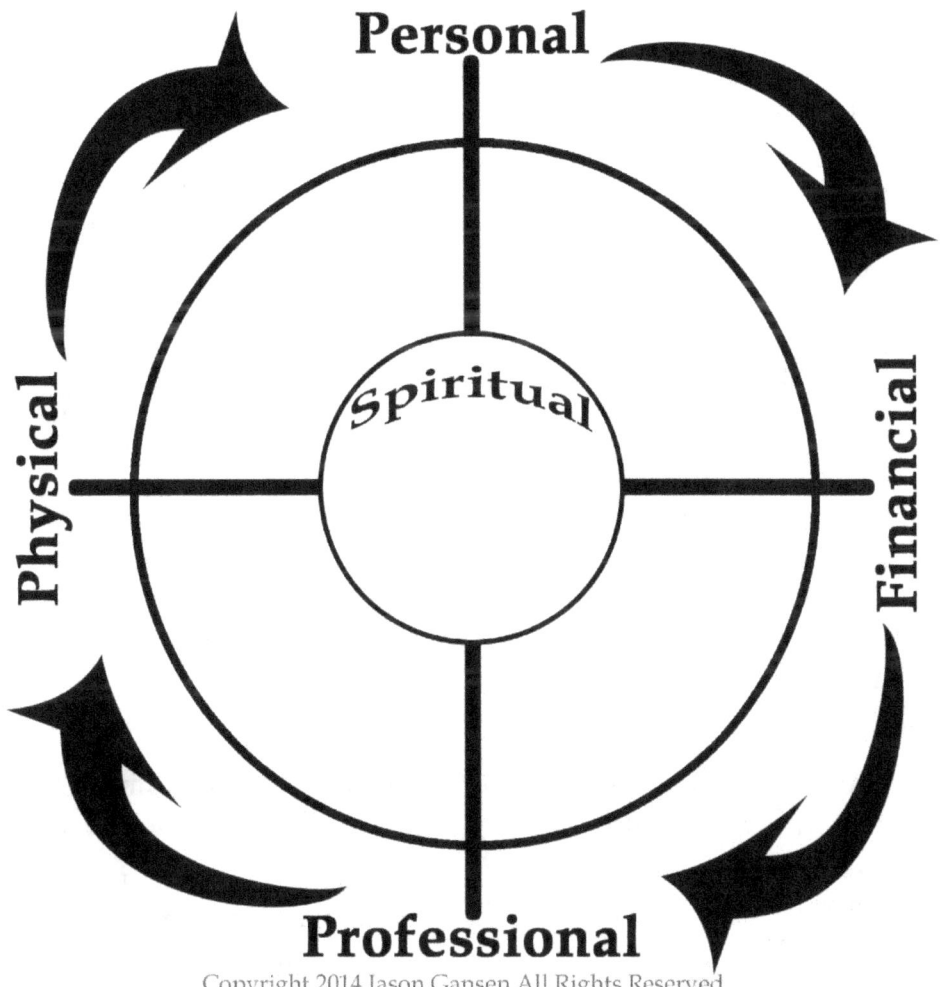

Figure 5

You are probably wondering what this has to do with motivation, goals, sales, or business success. Todd Ellingson, a friend and salesman, and I discovered several years ago that our sales day was directly correlated to our moods.

If we where happy, excited, inspired, in a good mood, or had a feeling of well-being, our sales for that day increased. If we were in a bad mood, sad, depressed, irritated, or mad, our sales decreased or dropped completely. On our bad days, it was better to go home than to ruin good sales leads.

I will give you an example: Let's say you have money in the bank, your bills are all paid, and you have a stable financial plan. Your career is soaring and you've been groomed for a move up in the company. You work out regularly, eat right, and have no medical issues. All is great except you and your spouse start fighting because of the long hours you spend away from home while you are at work or at the gym.

If you continue to fight with your spouse, your relationship with your spouse will begin to deteriorate or you will cut back on your hours at work and lose your promotion. You could stop going to the gym and your health could decline.

Once your health begins to decline, your drive could begin to slip, which causes a decrease in your financial well-being. Once your physical, professional, and financial balance starts to slip and move more toward family and your personal relationships, you may begin to fight with your spouse again because there is a decrease in financial security.

As your happiness decreases, you may stop spending time on yourself. You could fall into a deeper sense of religion and meditation to cope with the other areas in your life and lose your focus and balance. Another alternative could be that your spirituality could weaken altogether as your life begins to spiral downward.

> When you are trying to keep balance in your life, stay positive and always do the right thing. You won't have things hanging over your head bringing you bad karma if you are always making ethical and moral decisions.
>
> "Do good things and good things happen. Do bad things, bad things happen."
>
> -Denny Erickson

This might be an exaggerated example, but the scenarios are all the same in any off balance direction. This could be a happier version of what could happen as well. Depending on the situation, your life balance could result in total collapse and deep depression. Your relationship could end in divorce, your health could deteriorate, you could lose your job, and have financial destruction and increased debt.

Think about a time in your past that you had a deficiency in any one area: personal, financial, professional, physical, or spiritual. What happened to the other areas in your life? Did you see a surge in happiness or sadness? Did you try to compensate or over compensate in another area?

How about abundance in one area? Have you ever had extreme success or over-indulgence in one of the areas in your life? What happened to the balance in your life? Was anything else affected? Did you focus on one area as another was left out? What happened to your total life satisfaction?

Keeping perfect balance may be near impossible, but thankfully there are built in tolerances. As we move on to goals and goal setting in the next section, we will take a more in-depth look at the Life Balance illustration. Through goals and goal setting, your quest toward balance in your life will become a little easier to understand and manage.

Once you learn how to keep your life in balance and maintain a certain level of happiness or acceptance, your motivation levels should increase. Having additional motivation through happiness will also affect your life balance, resulting in a positive effect. Eventually, your life balance and motivation will perpetuate themselves.

Your Life In Balance Recap

1. Each area of your life affects the other in a positive or negative way.
2. Keeping your life in balance will increase your happiness and overall success.
3. Keeping your personal, financial, professional, and physical life in check while connecting it all together with spiritual goals will increase your life satisfaction.
4. Consider karma as a real force. Doing good things will produce the same in return.

Additional Resources & Links

1. Search your favorite search engine or on Youtube.com for "Your life in Balance" or "Life Balance Wheel" for articles, pictures, or videos.

Final Thoughts On Motivation

Your motivation almost always comes from a strong purpose. Your purpose is the reason why you are doing something. Dig really deep when searching for your "why." The deeper you dig, the stronger your motivation will be.

If you say, "I want to have more money," that could provide you with motivation. If you say, "I want to have more money to pay bills," would be even stronger. If you say, "I want to have more money to pay bills, so we don't have to struggle financially as much. Then, I won't have to work as hard. My parents always had to work extra hours when I was I was a kid, which made me miss them. I want to provide more for my children, so they don't cry themselves to sleep like I did." Now THAT is a motivating statement!

If you have a strong desire (you really want what you are setting out to achieve) and you have a definite purpose, your motivation will be at its highest level. Join in persistence, belief in your imminent success, and a plan with strong goals, you can't be stopped.

Section 2: Goals & Goal Setting

Luck vs. Goals

Let's go back to our discussion on luck from the beginning of the book. We discussed that your odds of becoming "lucky" increases with motivation and a little hard work. But this is only part of the equation.

I found it very interesting that when I was writing the motivation section of this book, I was very motivated! Talking and thinking about motivation day and night made me motivated. I thought about my motivation to write this book and how I could translate what I was feeling into something you as the reader could benefit from. As a result, I wrote almost every day.

After I finished the motivation section and transitioned to this section, something happened - I didn't practice what I was preaching. I had a run of "bad luck." I didn't write a single word for almost two months.

Why was all this stuff happening so I couldn't write this book and stay on my deadline? I thought luck or bad luck wasn't a tangible thing. Did I lose my motivation? Didn't I have the proper inspiration or research completed? Was I attracting bad things to happen that were worse than when I was writing the motivation section?

I stopped doing ONE thing I had been doing when I was working on the motivation section – *daily and weekly goal setting!* Sure, I still had my final publishing deadline, but only having a final completion date in the distant future did NOT produce the proper motivation. Only having a completion date won't work for you either.

It wasn't that I was having any different luck than usual.

> "The problem is not the problem. The problem is your attitude about the problem. Ultimately, you have complete control over whether you are happy or unhappy in life."
>
> -Jason Yoshino

Things happen to you, me, and to everybody all the time. People get sick, injured, end up in the hospital, have unexpected things come up, etc. and still manage to get things done.

I saw a quote on Facebook the other day that gave me the kick in the shorts I needed. "Life is 10% what happens to me and 90% of how I react to it." Charles R. Swindoll http://thinkexist.com/quotes/charles_r._swindoll/

Links & Additional Resources

1. Jason Yoshino (Energy Event Group) http://energyeventgroup.com/
2. http://thinkexist.com/quotes/charles_r._swindoll/

Why Set Goals?

All of us dream. We dream about the perfect job, a great vacation, a dream home, the perfect mate. Why does a small percent of the population always seem to attain their dreams and others don't? Successful people have motivation, set goals, watch for opportunities and act on them, turn a bad situation into a positive, and they believe they can achieve their goals.

In my book "How To Save Thousands: Do It Yourself!" I explain how I am able to accomplish, build, and fix things so I can save money. Simply put, I have the motivation. I set goals to accomplish the task and I truly believe I can do it. My motto is, "I'm smart enough to know how to figure it out, but dumb enough to not know I can't do it." Before taking on any project, you need to believe in yourself and your ability to complete the tasks that are needed. If you can't do the tasks, you must be able to delegate to someone that can.

You have a dream, the motivation, and you believe you can do it. The next step is to set your goal(s). To do this, a little planning is required. Don't be frightened by setting goals because most of us already set goals without even thinking about it. Napoleon Hill summarized it best, "A goal is a dream with a deadline."

A goal can be planned for years or it can be made on the spur of the moment. Todd Ellingson used to go door-to-door selling aerial photography. Sometimes he lost steam by the end of the day and wanted to go home, but needed to keep going. His solution was to make an impromptu goal. "I can't go home until I go to 5 more houses."

Todd's impromptu goal wasn't written and there wasn't a lot of thought put into it, but his goal had all the essential qualities of a successful plan. He had a task to complete, a dream, the motivation, a goal, and he believed he could do it. As a result, some of his biggest sales have come from those last 5 houses.

The previous section helped you realize and enhance what motivates you. Without a set goal, you still only have a dream and a desire to accomplish it, but having a well thought out goal will perpetuate your motivation into the stratosphere. With written goals, you can truly accomplish anything you set out to do.

Why Set Goals? Recap

1. Believe in your goals, have a strong desire, and believe in your ability to achieve them with your whole heart.
2. Goals need to be planned and a deadline set.
3. Short impromptu goals can be very motivational whether they are written or not.

Beginning Your Plan

The first step in goal setting is to know what the goal is. You will want to dig deep to find the true, underlying desire. Let's say your goal is to build shelves out of wood. Is your true goal or desire to build shelves or to make money? Are you more interested in the selling part or building part? Do you want something to occupy your time or become a corporation and mass produce your shelves some day? Your goals will be written very differently depending on what your dream is.

> "If you don't know where you are going, you'll end up someplace else."
>
> -Yogi Berra

If your dream is to occupy your time as a hobby, you probably won't write down your goal. If you plan to get to it when you have the time or only build a couple shelves, you don't have a deadline; therefore, a goal <u>doesn't</u> exist.

If your dream is to build the shelves as birthday presents, you have a deadline; therefore, a goal <u>does</u> exist. You know your dream (to build shelves), you have the motivation (personalized gift/save money), and you have a goal (everything combined, plus steps needed combined with a deadline), you believe you can do it, and you are taking advantage of an opportunity.

If you plan on turning your shelf building into a business to make money, you will need to do a lot more planning. You might need to purchase more equipment and hire employees. Your goals will need to range from short-term to long-term goals planned from daily up to 20 years. If your goals are not properly designed in this scenario, your business will turn into a hobby or won't get off the ground at all.

After you have established your desire, objective, or project, ask yourself again, "Is this the end goal or is this a step leading to the real, ultimate goal?" If you find that your answer to this question is a step leading to your goal, dig deeper. If you have defined the ultimate goal, you can continue to the next step.

> When dealing with a multitude of projects, staff, budget concerns, and obtaining the proper timely approvals, Tim Morris gives this advice, "Analyze your entire task list and individual goals first. Identify all of the individual pieces of information needed for each task, and gather the information you need in the quickest and most efficient way possible. Organize your data and assemble your team of qualified personnel to delegate responsibilities to. Discuss your deadlines and completion standards with your team and get busy with the project."

Tim Morris, a business manager at The Institute for Transportation, begins his goal setting by organizing his known tasks that need to be completed. He continues his plan by organizing his goals' completion in chronological order for each of his deadlines, and then delegates pieces of the goals to the qualified individuals for each task according to his staff's workload.

Tim has several goals and projects going at once with several deadlines. To keep organized, he keeps a project list and organizes it by his due dates. Tim states that his task list is a living document that is constantly being updated and revised. As projects and deadlines change or when new projects are added to his list, he can get an immediate, high-level overview of any foreseeable conflicts.

Without daily, weekly, monthly, and annual goal and budget setting and acquiring the proper approval for projects, Mr. Morris could fall behind on his project's completion deadlines. It wouldn't take long before his projects were in total collapse.

> "He who fails to plan is planning to fail"
>
> -Winston Churchill

If you don't <u>write</u> <u>down</u> your tasks and goals, it won't take long before you are missing deadlines and forgetting things that need to be done.

To-Do List

Time
A: Requires attention within 1 week
B: Requires attention within 1 month
C: To be started after a month

Resources
1: Within budget and resources available
2: Funds needed or help required
3: Resources not readily available

#: Order of completion

#	List	Time	Resources

Copyright 2014 Jason Gansen All Rights Reserved.

Figure 6

I have created a helpful To-Do List (Figure 6) worksheet that will assist you in organizing your tasks that need to be completed so you can prioritize all your goals.

To-Do List Instructions

1. The check mark on the left column is used to check off completed items.
2. The List column is to write down the name of your goal/task/project that needs to be completed.
3. The Time column is to be given an A, B, or C rating for each task.
   a. A = requires attention within 1 week
   b. B = requires attention within 1 month
   c. C = To be started after a month or no specific start date required
4. The Resources column is to be given a 1, 2, or 3 rating for each task.
5. 1 = The goal/project/task/to-do is within your budget and resources you have available
6. 2 = Funds are needed or help is required
7. 3 = Resources are not readily available and/or may be difficult to procure.
8. The Order column allows you to prioritize your list. Number your to-do's 1, 2, 3, 4... through however many items you have. The Time and Resources columns will help you prioritize your list. Remember, this list is based on when the project needs to <u>start</u>, *not* on the <u>deadline</u>.
   a. Your A1 ratings should be your first and easiest items to complete and need to be completed soon. A2 and A3 items also need to begin within the week, but may require additional, immediate attention if your resources are not readily available. Since these items need to be completed within a week, you may want to begin your A3 items before anything else so you allow yourself enough time to obtain the funds and/or help you need to begin the project.
   b. Your B1 items should be the next items to complete followed by B2 and B3. Again, if your B3 items will take additional time to acquire the resources needed to complete the project, you may want to list B3 before B1 or B2 so you can start working on obtaining those resources.

c. Your last numbered items will be C1, C2, and C3. These items are required to begin beyond a month and should be listed accordingly.

You will need to use your best judgment when considering your prioritization. Just because an item is listed as an A1 doesn't mean it has to be first. A C3 might be the first thing you want to start.

Let's say you want to buy a house and you plan to remodel it in two months from now. Although your project of buying a house and remodeling it won't begin for a while (prioritized as a C3), you may need to get approved for a loan before that can happen. Since it could take a month or more to get approved, you may need to begin that process immediately. In this example, you might have incorrectly identified your project. It may seem like the goal should start in two months, but in reality, it should be listed as an A3 or a B3.

This list is subjective to your beliefs and internal priorities, but will give you a great guide to organize the things you have going on in your life. Make sure to revisit your to-do list often. This should be a fluid, working document that changes on a daily basis as you add new items, complete others, secure resources, and start dates/deadlines approach or expire. View the example in (Figure 7) to see what a completed To-Do List would look like.

	To-Do List			
	Time A: Requires attention within 1 week B: Requires attention within 1 month C: To be started after a month	Resources 1: Within budget and resources available 2: Funds needed or help required 3: Resources not readily available		
✓	List	Time	Resources	Order
	Mow the lawn	A	1	2
	Do the dishes	A	1	1
	Meet with marketing companies	A	1	3
	Begin new marketing plan	B	2	5
	Get a home loan with additional resources for remodeling	B	3	4
	Hire help for remodel	C	2	6
	Close on home	C	3	7
	Begin remodel	C	3	8
	Copyright 2014 Jason Gansen All Rights Reserved.			

Figure 7

After you have completed your To-Do List and identified the goals that have priority, the final step before you begin writing out your goals is to have a group discussion. Everyone involved with the goal or project should be able to answer the following questions-

Group Discussion Questions

1. Has the goal been properly identified?
    a. Is the goal just a step toward the bigger picture or is it the underlying and ultimate goal?
2. Does everyone involved agree upon the start date and deadline?
3. Has the proper resources needed been identified and allocated with proper approval? i.e. staff, equipment, materials needed, funding, etc.
    a. If not, who needs to give approval?
    b. Who is responsible for acquiring the proper resources?
4. Who is the project manager and responsible for the project?
5. What completion standards are there, if any?

6. What compromises need to be made or can be made to satisfy everyone involved?
7. Has everyone involved been included in the discussion?
8. Has a final agreement been made by everyone involved?

Beginning Your Plan Recap

1. Know what your true goal or desire is.
2. Organize your goals by start date, due date, importance, and time required to complete the goal.
3. Creating a To-Do List to organize your projects by time and resources will allow you to organize them in a logical manner.
4. Delegate responsibilities as needed to qualified individuals to accomplish your goals more efficiently.

Additional Resources & Links

1. Free download for To-do list
   a. http://www.howtoevolveyourbusiness.com/

The Goal Setting Process

When creating your goals, you should always write your goals using the S.M.A.R.T. technique or format. Your goals should be –

S.M.A.R.T. Goals

1. Specific
   a. What are you trying to achieve? Is it an income level, an award, a task, an achievement, a project, an invention to solve a problem, a chore, etc. List out specifically what you are looking to accomplish.
2. Measurable
   a. What completion standards are you shooting for? If it is an income level, what is that number? Use an indicator that will provide you with success, failure, or achievement of your goal.
3. Action-Oriented

a. Steps or items that need to be followed to achieve the goal. What are the things you or someone else needs to do to have success?
4. <u>R</u>ealistic
   a. Is the goal something you believe you can do? If you have a goal to walk on Mars, chances are it won't happen. But if you are an astronaut or have established a career path to become an astronaut, walking on Mars becomes a little more realistic. If you don't believe you can achieve your goal, it won't happen.

> "Whether you think you can, or you think you can't -- you're right."
>
> -Henry Ford

5. <u>T</u>ime and Resource Constrained
   a. What deadline exists, when does each step have to be done, and how much time and money are you willing to invest?

The next step to writing down your goal is to consider which format you want to use. Some people can write out their goals in freeform, while others need to follow a format. I have used both methods and have found either to work for me. For simple or daily goals, I recommend freeform. Freeform is the least time consuming, while longer-term goals or complex goals require a formatted structure so you don't leave anything out. You will need to discover for yourself which method is right for you.

An example of a freeform goal might be, "Appointment tomorrow at 3:00 p.m. with John Doe in my office. Begin prep for appointment at 2:30 p.m. by getting client file out, look over the proposal, print required paperwork."

This goal has a time, date, person responsible, a belief the task is achievable, motivation, an opportunity, and action required. There is a lot of stuff involved with this goal either directly or indirectly implied, but in a organized couple of sentences.

Freeform is as simple as an entry in your day planner or calendar or a task list for the following day(s) or week's worth of activities that need to be accomplished.

For complex or more involved goals, I have used a goal sheet for the past fifteen years with a great deal of success. I have also required my students and employees to use a similar goal sheet.

COMPLETION DATE 5/15/2015	Specific Project/Goal Name/Objective: Obtain Rock Star Status Award by earning $100,000 commissioned sales selling 100 widgets in one year by increasing marketing, making new contacts, and setting 300 prospect appointments.
Person(s) Responsible: **Me**	WIIFM: Earn prestigious company award and increased income, build a foundation for a successful business, develop habits for future success, be able to take my family on a vacation with the additional income earned.

Action Plan/Steps/Completion	Deadline:
☐ Start Date	5/15/2014
☐ Set 3 appointments	Daily
☐ Contact 5 marketing companies to set and hold appointments for creating a marketing strategy and budget	5/22/2014
☐ Select marketing company and secure marketing budget	5/24/2014
☐ Implement new marketing plan	5/25/2014
☐ Complete company training course to increase sales skills	1 day 5/27/2014
☐ Plan weekly activities for the following week (EOB = end of business day)	Every Friday by EOB
☐ Success indicator: 50 widgets sold or $50,000 commission by November 1, 2014	
☐ Evaluate and adjust action plan according to actual sales and projections	Weekly

Contingency Plan for Obstacles/Restrictions
☐ Sick time/leave for self or kids - increase set appointments daily to 6 once returned or make calls from home while out. Have manager or secretary help with calls, scheduling, holding appointments
☐ Not on target for selling 100 widgets - cross sell clients, up-sell, obtain referrals
☐ Marketing plan not working - track marketing and sales numbers, re-evaluate and change methods of marketing - evaluate daily and weekly numbers
☐ Budget runs out of marketing dollars - look for free or less expensive marketing ideas, make sure to follow marketing plan budget was based on from the beginning

Copyright 2014 Jason Gansen All Rights Reserved.

Figure 8

Please look over the example goal sheet (Figure 8). Pay special attention to the topic box titles and look over the example entries for each box. This quick overview will allow you to better comprehend the explanations of each topic box as I explain them.

Goal Worksheet Category Outline:

1. Completion Date
2. Specific Project/Goal Name/Objective
3. Person(s) Responsible
4. WIIFM (What's In It For Me?)
5. Action Plan/Steps/Completion Standards and Deadline
6. Contingency Plan For Obstacles/Restrictions

Goal Worksheet Explanation (Figure 9):

1. Completion Date: One of the most important pieces to the puzzle of goal setting is your deadline. Your deadline drives your goal forward and is the finish line. Remember, a goal without a deadline is only a dream. I wanted the completion date to be the most visible thing on your goal sheet, so I put it at the top. Write your goal's completion date in big numbers and only put the final date in this spot.
2. Specific Project/Goal Name/Objective: This section is where you will put your main project name, goal, objective, or outcome you desire in S.M.A.R.T. format. You should make this a high level, yet specific sentence or two. There are 4 items that should be included:
   a. What you are trying to attain or achieve, i.e., "Achieve Rock Star Status Award"
   b. What needs to happen or high-level completion standard or target number to achieve goal, i.e., "by earning $100,000 commissioned sales selling 100 widgets"
   c. High-level end date listed as a week, month, less than a year, etc., i.e., "in one year"
   d. High-level action required to achieve the goal, i.e., "by increasing marketing, making new contacts, and setting 300 prospect appointments."
3. Person(s) Responsible: Person, persons, or group responsible for the completion of the goal.
4. WIIFM: What's In It For Me? This is your driving force, your motivation, what you will get out of the successful completion of the goal. You should try to incorporate one or several of your top motivators. Creating a dream board for

your reward for completing your goal is another approach to motivate your success.

5. Action Plan/Steps/Completion Standards and Deadline: A Specific list of items that need to be completed. Project indicators showing that the project is on target for completion on time. Items that will provide evidence the goal is correctly being performed to a set standard. Each item in the list should have a deadline of either a specific date or as a repeating item such as: daily, weekly, monthly, etc.

   a. Contingency Plan for Obstacles/Restrictions: List obstacles to your goal and your contingency plan to overcome the obstacles. Also, write down potential obstacles that could happen and a game plan to resolve the issue if it occurs. Read the next chapter, Obstacles To Goals for further information.

COMPLETION DATE	Specific Project/Goal Name/Objective:
Final Date for Project/Goal Completion	In S.M.A.R.T. format - Name of project or goal to complete I.E. Weightloss, Widget project, publish book, Clean yard, Replace kitchen cabinets, etc.
Person(s) Responsible: Who will help me complete project, is it me alone, or people I can deligate to I.E. Me; John, Tracy, Bob, and me	WIIFM: What will I get out of this? What is the benefits? Where is my motivation coming from? Use my top motivators if possible I.E. I will feel better and be healthier, I will help other people, I will make $X bonus, I will keep my job, I will get more projects in the future that could lead to pay increase/promotion, etc.

Action Plan/Steps/Completion	Deadline:
☐ Start Date	
How will I know when the goal is completed? What needs to be accomplished? What indicators need to be met? What are the steps that need to be completed and by what date? I.E. I will lose 10 lbs in 30 days, the book will be available for purchase by April 1, production for widgets will be able to begin/shipping/product placement in stores, etc by April 1st. List each step and the deadline for each step. If there are any indicators to know when each step is made or completion standards, list them as well.	

Contingency Plan for Obstacles/Restrictions	
☐ List of obstacles or issues that could occur during the project and what can be done to counteract the issue. I.e. Run out of time - recruit more help/delegate/extend deadline/lessen completion standards. Run out of money - request extension of credit or increase budget/scrap project/drop X, Y, and Z from project, etc.	

Copyright 2014 Jason Gansen All Rights Reserved.

Figure 9

COMPLETION DATE	Specific Project/Goal Name/Objective:
Person(s) Responsible:	WIIFM:

Action Plan/Steps/Completion   Deadline:
☐ Start Date
☐
☐
☐
☐
☐
☐
☐
☐
☐
☐
☐
☐

Contingency Plan for Obstacles/Restrictions
☐
☐
☐
☐
☐
☐
☐
☐
☐
☐

Copyright 2014 Jason Gansen All Rights Reserved.

Figure 10

The Goal Setting Process Recap

1. Use the S.M.A.R.T. goal setting technique
   a. Specific
   b. Measurable
   c. Action-Oriented
   d. Realistic
   e. Time and Resource Constrained
2. Freeform goals are written out in simple terms but require:
   a. A time
   b. A date
   c. Person responsible
   d. A belief the task is achievable
   e. Motivation
   f. An opportunity
   g. Action is required
3. Freeform goals can be written down anywhere as long as it is easily accessible.
4. Using a goal worksheet will help organize your goals much better. A goal worksheet is very detailed and will help you achieve your goals more accurately and timely than the freeform or any other method.

Additional Resources & Links

1. Free download for goal worksheets
   a. http://www.howtoevolveyourbusiness.com

Obstacles To Goals

If you are like me, I have always been able to think clearer looking from the outside in, than when I'm in a situation. This is also evident if you have ever found it easier to give someone advice on a problem they are having than if you are in the same situation yourself. Because this is true, try to identify any issues that could arise that prevent you from completing your goal and its potential solution. That

> "Obstacles are those frightful things you see when you take your eyes off your goal."
>
> -Henry Ford

way, if something comes up that is blocking your goal, you can look back and see the solutions you have already thought of.

Obstacle Considerations

1. You won't always think of everything that could happen.
2. You won't always have the correct solution.
3. You will provide yourself with a starting point to overcome obstacles that arise.

When thinking about potential obstacles to your goals, consider the following common issues you could come across and a few ideas to overcome them:

Obstacles and Possible Solutions

1. Broad based obstacles – obstacles that encompass a large subject, topic, or field. Broad based obstacles could affect a large number of people. Wars, government, taxes, death, mother nature, plagues, epidemics, depression/recession, etc. Broad based obstacles are completely out of your control; therefore, will be more difficult or impossible to overcome. (If you figure out a legal way out of taxes or how to cheat death… let me know, okay?)
    a. Obstacles that are out of your control – If you are in the construction business, you can't control the weather. Let's say you have to build a house and have a specific deadline, it has been rainy or windy for months. What are your options? You may have to extend the deadline or suck it up and do as much as you can in the elements. Maybe you could construct a temporary tent around the area you are working on?
2. Specific obstacles – Not enough time, money, equipment, or resources, not having enough knowledge for the project, and short on help could be examples of specific obstacles. You could hire more help, manage delegation more efficiently, get a loan, drop some of the unnecessary activities in your life, buy or rent equipment, and get the proper training you or your employees need.

3. Physical obstacles – Could occur from injuries, being tired or worn-out, out of shape, over weight, malnourished, illness, etc. Physical obstacles are a reminder from your body to take care of yourself or that something is wrong. If you have physical obstacles, you may need to take some time off, hire additional help, or see a professional.
4. Psychological barriers – Not thinking you're are good enough, lack of motivation, time management issues, lack of self-confidence, depression, hyperactivity, obsession/compulsion, and a multitude of psychological disorders could be a psychological barrier. Training, reading this book, writing down your goals, having obstacle contingency plans, etc. could help reduce or eliminate this type of obstacle. Some neurological disorders may require seeing a specialist and/or medication.
5. Inner obstacles – Inner obstacles would be similar to physical or psychological barriers. This type of obstacle may or may not be something you control. Time management, not believing in yourself, not being motivated, and not properly planning the project are things that are within your control and things you can change.
6. Outer obstacles – Outer obstacles are caused by other people or things. You may or may not be able to control them, but you can manage them. Things like employees not showing up for work or quitting, and tools or equipment malfunctioning would be good examples. Outer obstacles, as in these examples, could be managed by having extra resources available: temp. Agency, part time help, extra tools and equipment, or utilizing a tool rental company.

Keep in mind when you are writing down potential obstacles and your contingency plans that they are only potentials! You should not obsess about what ifs and would coulds. Spend a little time thinking about what your plan is and move on.

Sometimes the best way to overcome obstacles is to revise your goal or come up with a new goal. You could even go in a different direction than what you initially intended.

At the beginning of the Goals section, I told you a story about Todd Ellingson. His goal was to go to as many houses door-to-door as he could and complete one sales packet a day. His obstacles where people not being home, people not giving him the opportunity to show what he had to offer, frustration, and fatigue.

His contingency plan was to create an impromptu goal. It was unwritten, on the spot, but very effective. "I can't quit today until I go to 5 more houses." He didn't care if he sold to them or even if they let him in the house. He just needed 5 more houses, then he could reward himself by being done for the day.

In S.M.A.R.T. goal format, it was perfect and got him through the end of his day.

Todd's S.M.A.R.T. Goal:

1. Specific: 5 more houses whether he sold or not.
2. Measurable: Todd knew how many extra houses he had went to and how many he had left.
3. Action Oriented: He had to drive to the house, walk up to the door, and give his presentation.
4. Realistic: He completely and entirely believed he could go to the houses. Since he didn't say he had to sell to 5 more houses, he knew that it wouldn't take very long since some of the people wouldn't want anything to do with his product.
5. Time and Resource Constrained: He had to complete the goal that evening.
6. He also included the motivation or WIIFM (What's in it for me): He got to go home or to the hotel to relax when he was done.

The Circle of Control

I stressed about a lot of stuff in my early adulthood. I worried about everything. What I began to realize and what a manager pointed out to me, most of my day spent on worrying was about things that where beyond my control or would never happen in the first place!

I wasted so much time worrying, that it consumed me. My manager, Denny Erickson showed me the chart below (Figure 11) called "The Circle of Control."

If issues or obstacles arose that were within my control or could be influenced by me, then I needed to figure out a solution and move on. If it was beyond my control, I needed to try to find someone that could control the issue, change my goal, or move on.

My manager taught me to put little time and effort into things that haven't happened or may never happen. The extra brainpower I freed up allowed me to focus my energy on things I could control. I could get more done with a higher efficiency.

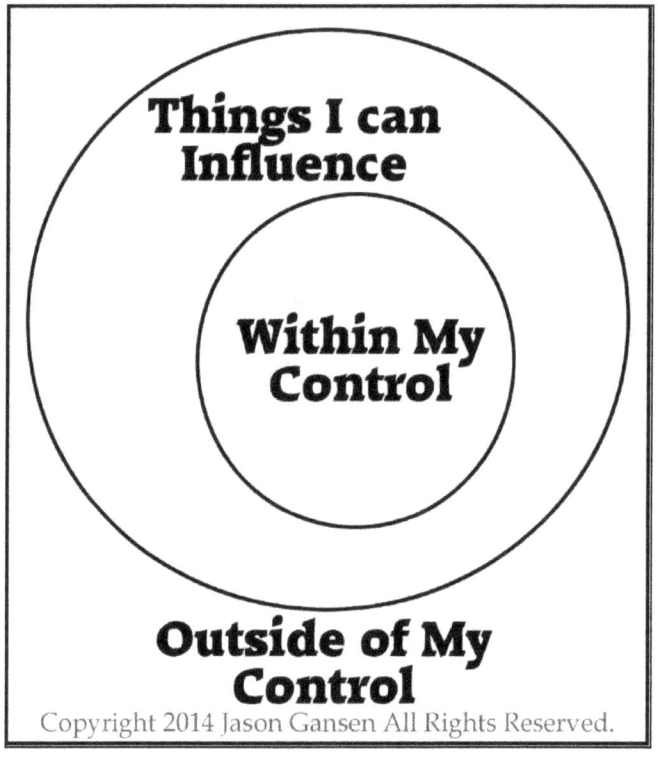

Figure 11

The next time you are faced with obstacles or worry ask yourself the following:

1. Can I control this?

2. Can I influence the outcome?
3. Is this outside my control?
4. Is there someone that can help with the issue?
5. Has this already happened?
6. Is there a high probability this will never happen?

Pretender Offenders

Sometimes your obstacles may not be obstacles at all. Adjusting your motivation or goals may provide a resolution. Your disruptive feelings toward your goals could be something entirely different.

Ask yourself the following:

1. Low Motivation – Do you daydream about what you could be doing rather than completing the task? Would you rather be doing anything else other than your goal? Did you skip the WIIFM section of your goal setting worksheet? Are you procrastinating your project? Do you feel like there are a lot of other things that are way more important to get done first than your goal?
    a. If you answered, "yes" to some or all of these questions, you need to spend some time on finding your motivation for the project you are working on. Find a strong "What's In It For Me" that will get you going. If you have tried using positive motivation to no avail, try using negative motivation. "If I don't get this done, I will get fired… or I won't get my next raise."
2. Low Goals – Do you know exactly what you want or want to achieve? Do you have trouble taking that first step toward your dream job or lifestyle? Do you read a lot of self help books or attend high impact seminars?
    a. If you answered, "yes" to some or all of these questions, you need to spend some time thinking about what goals would help you attain your dreams or turn your dreams into a goal. In this scenario, you have high motivation, but low goals or weak goals. Focus on creating S.M.A.R.T. goals and writing out your plans. Spend some time thinking about the steps you need to take to achieve

your dreams and put a deadline for each step. Find a final deadline and stick to it.
3. Goal Scattering – Do you have a lot of motivation and a lot of goals? Do you often find yourself starting one thing and moving on to another before the first goal is completed? Do you have trouble finishing all your projects?
   a. If you answered, "yes" to some or all of these questions, you could have too many irons in the fire. Complete a To-Do list (Figure 6) and prioritize your goals. Organize them in the order they need to be completed and by when they need to be started if they will take awhile. Try to focus on one or two things at a time, complete them, and then move on. I used to be terrible at this. I would start working on some papers, find something else I needed to work on, and put the first project on hold while continuing with what I just found or thought of. The cycle would repeat when I came across something else. I had a lot of partially done items and very few or no completed ones. I started a new philosophy, "If I pick it up, I work on it until it's done." This can be a real challenge, but try to stick to one thing until its completed then move on.
4. Over-Trained – Do you spend more time reading or watching videos that will help you achieve your goals than actually doing them? Do you feel like you will start working on your goal when you are completely ready, but never feel ready enough no matter how much info you take in? Can you talk about what needs to be done all day? Do you find it easier to tell other people how to complete the goal than it is to do it yourself?
   a. If you answered, "yes" to some or all of these questions, you could be over-trained and over-prepared. Go back to your goal worksheet, which I am sure is completely filled out, and go to the first step and _DO_ it!! Set _firm_ deadlines and don't allow yourself to go past them. Become a person of _action_. Nothing will happen until you do something.
5. Under Trained – Are you trying to work on your goal, but have no idea how to complete the next step? Do you find

yourself saying, "I know how to do it (or I understand it), but I couldn't explain it to anyone." Are you spending a lot of time asking others what to do next? Do you spend a lot of time thinking about hypothetical things that could happen, but probably never will? Do you often have other people tell or ask you, "Just let me do it," "Do you need some help?" or "Do you want me to help you?"

    a. If you answered, "yes" to some or all of these questions, you could be under trained. If you are under trained, seek additional help on your subject area. You can read, watch videos, enlist in a training course online, take a college course, get help from someone that is trained in the area, or ask your manager for help.

Obstacles happen to everyone. Don't stress about it or let it consume you. Your goal could be impaired depending on how you prepare or how you react. Just give yourself a plan you can follow and a direction to go. Remember: "Life is 10% what happens to me and 90% of how I react to it." (Charles R. Swindoll) My personal favorite quote is, "Shit happens, build a bridge and get over it."

> "When you mess up… take the mess up head on! …Address the mess-up quickly. Address, move on, and always be solution focused and forward thinking!
>
> -Ryan Thomas

Obstacles To Goals Recap

1. Creating a contingency plan for your obstacles will help you overcome them faster if they occur.
2. The different types of obstacles that could occur are: Broad based, specific, physical, psychological, inner, outer obstacles.
3. Some obstacles require a revision of your goal or a new goal.
4. Don't waste time worrying. Are you worrying about things that are within your control, within your influence, or beyond your control?

5. Are your obstacles real obstacles or pretender offenders: Low motivation, low goals, goal scattering, or caused by being over-trained, or under-trained?
6. When an obstacle occurs, tackle the obstacle head on and move on.

Additional Resources & Links

1. Download a free copy of The Circle Of Control:
   a. http://www.howtoevolveyourbusiness.com

Your Balance In Life – Goal Setting

We began our discussion on life balance in the Motivation section under the "Your Life In Balance" chapter. You should have a better understanding of how a balanced life can affect your motivation and success on a personal and professional level. The next step is to learn how to set your personal goals to keep your life in check. Look at the example chart on the next page (Figure 12).

Keep in mind this is just one way to look at balancing your life. This is only one of many types of Life Balance wheels. If you want other examples and different types of wheels, go to your favorite search engine online and search for "Your Life In Balance." Look at the images and web pages. There is a lot of good information out there. The other versions have the same basic core elements, but have variants that you could find helpful.

My goal is to help you increase success. If you feel more of a connection using something else, go for it. Hopefully this will at least get you pointed in the right direction and you realize the importance of getting your life in balance.

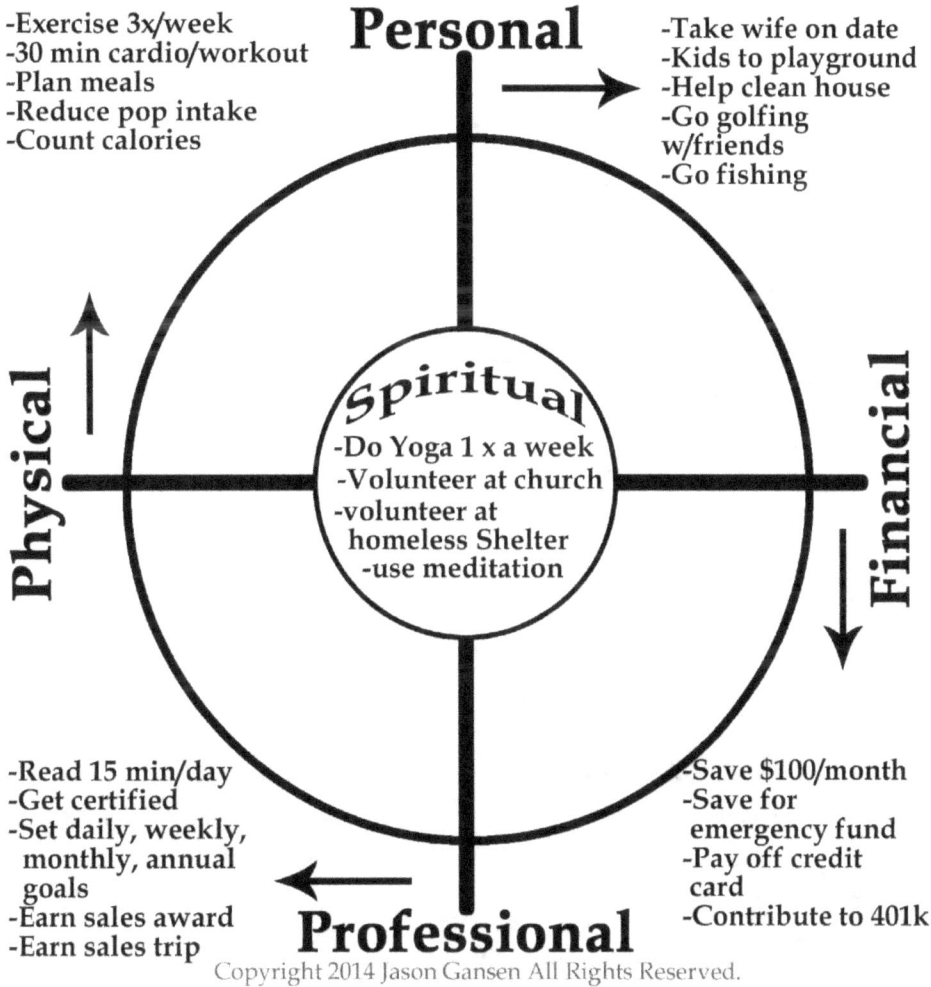

Figure 12

Each of the four main areas of your life: Personal, Financial, Professional, and Physical are tied together by your spiritual well-being. In this example, I have used the following goals:

Personal:

1. Take wife on date
2. Take kids to playground
3. Help clean the house
4. Go golfing with friends
5. Go fishing

Financial:

1. Save $100/month
2. Save for emergency fund
3. Pay off credit card
4. Contribute to 401k

Professional:

1. Read 15 minutes per day
2. Get certified
3. Set daily, weekly, monthly, and annual goals
4. Earn sales award
5. Earn sales trip

Physical:

1. Exercise 3 times per week
2. 30 minutes of cardio per workout
3. Plan meals
4. Reduce Pop intake
5. Count calories

Spiritual:

1. Do Yoga 1 time per week
2. Volunteer at church
3. Volunteer at a homeless shelter
4. Use Meditation

These are only examples and may or may not work for you, but will give you a starting point to think about. Take a look at your own life and what goals would complete your balance.

Some life balance goals may require a goal worksheet, and some may not. Reducing your pop intake probably needs more self-control and discipline than a lengthy plan. Earning a sales trip, on the other hand, will definitely require an extensive plan and goal sheet.

Here are some items to consider for helping find peace and add balance to your life for each category. Try to list 5 daily habits for each area of your life and review your list every day. Fill out your own chart if needed (Figure 13).

Personal:

1. Activities you can do with people important in your life
2. Hobbies you can do by yourself or with family
3. Spending time with the important people in your life
4. Organize or clean your house, apartment, garage, etc.
5. Things you can do to help your significant other
6. Communicating with your significant other
7. Take a vacation or stay-cation

Financial:

1. Evaluate your personal financial goals
2. Enlist the help of a financial professional
3. Create a balance sheet with your income, investments, equity, bills, and debt
4. Evaluate your retirement goals
5. Read books, watch videos, or attend a seminar by a financial expert
6. Ask yourself where you want to be in 5, 10, or 20 years and at retirement.
7. What donations would you like to make? What charities are important to you?
8. What are your savings goals? What items are you saving for?

Professional:

1. What goals does your manager have for you?
2. Where do you want to go in the company?
3. What are your company goals, mission, vision, and values? What can you do to align yourself with them?
4. What awards or bonuses can you earn?
5. What certifications can you earn or training can you take?

6. You can read, watch videos, attend seminars, and audio training

Physical:

1. What is the ideal weight you want to be? What weight is healthy for your height? What is your body fat percentage and where should you be?
2. What are your eating habits? Are you eating balanced meals? What is your caloric intake? What supplements/vitamins are appropriate for your lifestyle?
3. You can exercise, cardiovascular training, use a trainer, utilize cross training, use a home gym or video exercise programs. What gym do you want to go to, etc.
4. What medical conditions need to be addressed and get under control?
5. Are you getting regular physicals by a trained medical professional?
6. Are you taking any medication? Could any of the medications you are taking be interfering with other medications?
7. What other items could improve your health?

Spiritual:

1. What do you consider calming and relaxing?
2. What are your religious beliefs?
3. What charities do you support or would like to support?
4. Have you ever tried meditation?
5. Do you like getting massages?
6. Do you practice prayer, attend religious services, donate your time to help your church, read scripture, or have you joined a prayer group, etc.
7. You could take a walk on the beach, go hiking, spend time in the woods, climb a mountain, watch a sunset, or do anything else you would consider a spiritual and calming experience.

Your Balance in Life – Goal Setting Recap

1. Having a balanced life will increase your motivation.

2. Set 5 goals for each area of your life: Personal, Financial, Professional, Physical, and Spiritual.
3. Look at your life balance goals every day and revise them as needed.

Additional Resources & Links

1. Search for "your life in balance" or "balance wheel" or "life balance" on your favorite search engine for additional links, pictures, different types of Life Balance Wheels, and videos.
2. Link for free download of a Life Balance Wheel
    a. http://howtoevolveyourbusiness.com/
3. Here is a blank copy of a "Your Life In Balance" chart. You can also draw it out on a piece of paper. If you want a printed version, go to my website for a free download:
    a. http://howtoevolveyourbusiness.com/

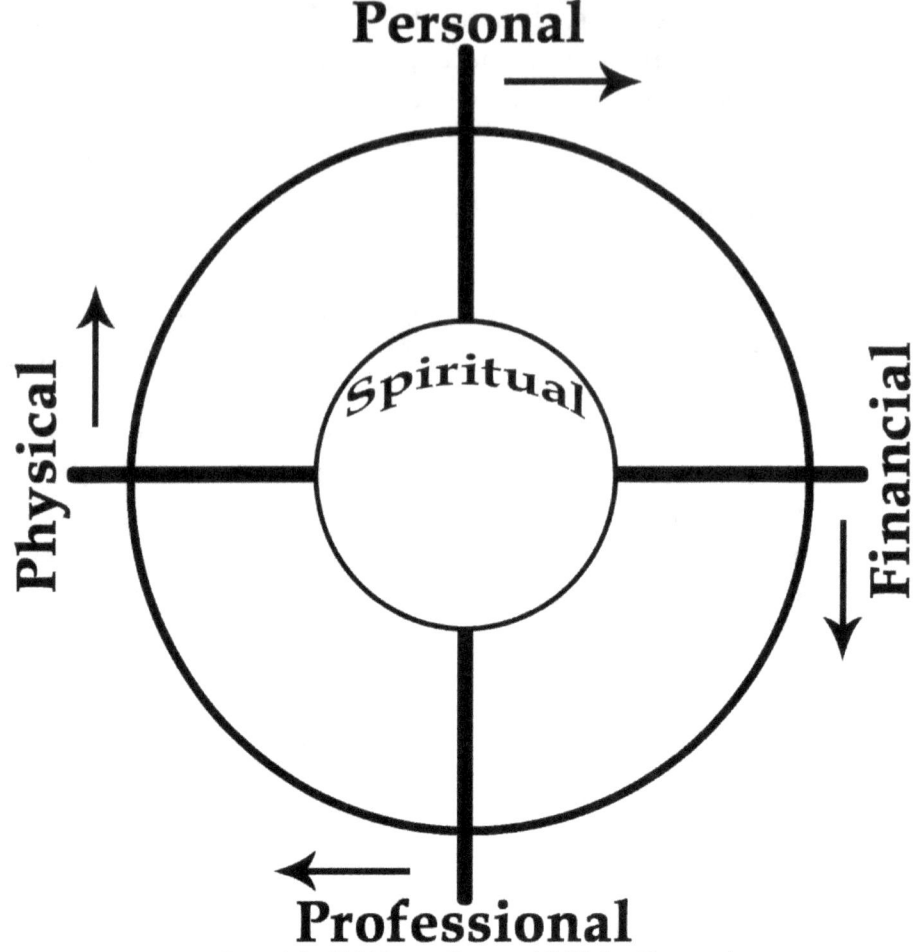

Copyright 2014 Jason Gansen All Rights Reserved.

Figure 13

What Goals Should I Have?

Where do you start if you don't know where to begin? At the beginning of this book, I gave you one of the best quotes I've ever heard. Albert E.N. Gray originally addressed the NALU in 1940 with the Common Denominator of Success and it has been a timeless rule for success ever since. It states, "The secret of success of every man who has ever been successful – lies in the fact that he formed the habit of doing things that failures don't like to do."

If you are having trouble getting started, or already well on your way, you will highly benefit by finding someone that can help you learn the habits of their success.

Emulate The Habits Of:

1. A mentor
2. Become a part of a mastermind group
3. Someone that has accomplished what you are working toward
4. Someone successful
5. Someone who is where you want to be
6. Someone that has earned the salary you want
7. An instructor that knows the path to success

A successful businessman from my hometown said, "If you want $50,000 in the bank, talk to someone that has $50,000 or more in the bank and learn from them. If you want a job that pays $100,000 a year, learn from someone that earns $100,000 a year. You should learn from and hang around people you want to be like.

You become like those you associate with. This works in a positive or negative manner. If you hang around drug addicts, troublemakers, or alcoholics, you will start acting the same way.

Once you find a successful person you can emulate, learn what they do on a daily basis. What have they done to become successful? What are their habits? Who do they hang around? What education have they received? Do they read, attend seminars, meet with other successful businessmen, and listen to success CD's or audio files?

Study what these people do and make habits out of their habits. If you are in sales, become a student of sales. What habits are a part of a successful salesman's day? The following examples are some habits to get you going –

Successful Habits:

1. They make prospecting calls.
2. They find new sales leads.
3. They get referrals.
4. They answer the phone and return calls in a timely manner.
5. They do what they say when they say it.
6. They believe in their product or service.
7. They do things that are difficult when others won't.
8. They take chances, but make educated decisions.
9. They have a positive attitude.
10. They are students of their product or service and they teach clients so the client can make an informed purchase.
11. They are ethical.
12. They don't break laws and industry regulations.

What Goals Should I Have? Recap

1. Successful people make habits out of the things failures are not willing to do.
2. Find someone you want to learn from and emulate them.
3. You become like the people you are around.
4. Discover the habits of successful people and follow their lead.

Additional Resources & Links

1. You can purchase a copy of "The Common Denominator of Success" by Albert E.N. Gray online or do a search on the Internet to download the PDF for free.

Managing Your Goals

Your plans should include short, mid, and long-term goals. Your short-term goals will include daily, weekly, and monthly goals. Your mid-term goals should be from six month to a year. Long-term goals are broken

> "I am constantly working on my goals and always have short, mid, and long-term goals planned out for my business."
>
> -Tom Wullstein

down into 5, 10, 20-year goals, and for retirement.

You should monitor the progress of your goals frequently and have goal indicators in place to know when you are ahead, behind, or on target for completion. You need to know where you are and where you are going at all times.

Do you remember the quote from Yogi Berra at the beginning of the goals section from this book? "If you don't know where you are going, you'll end up someplace else." I've also heard the quote as "If you don't know where you are going, you won't know if you've arrived." Live, eat, and breath your goals and you will find success. Learn to revise your goals as often as you need to achieve victory with anything your mind can believe in.

Keeping track of and managing many goals could become overwhelming. Here are some techniques you can do to manage them easier. I would recommend only using 1 or 2 methods. If you use more than that, you will lose track of where you put each goal. The confusion created by looking in several places will cause you to reduce or eliminate your success for completion.

> "What the mind of man can conceive and believe, it can achieve"
>
> -Napoleon Hill

How To Keep Track Of Your Goals

1. Use a day planner. The last thing you should do before you go home for the day is to write down your goals/to-do list for the next day. List out your goals at the bottom of the day column for tomorrow in your day planner. Reviewing your goals/to-do list for that day should be the first thing you do when you get to work in the morning. There is no need to repeat items that already have a time slot during the day. You can also use your day planner to list start dates, schedule checkpoints to evaluate your progress at certain stages during your projects, and deadlines. In addition, I had a three ring binder type day planner that had a tab for goals with blank sheets of paper I could write my to-do lists.

2. Create a goals binder. A goals binder is a three ring binder where you can keep all your current, future, and ongoing goal worksheets. You can also keep blank goal and to-do sheets in the inside pouch or under its own tab. You can keep your to-do lists, weekly progress sheets, motivation sheets, dream boards, etc. under their own tabs.
3. Use a smart phone app. There are a lot of paid and free apps out there that will help you write, track, and manage your goals. I don't personally use any of these, but some of the ones I looked at for this book looked really good. I do; however, currently use a notepad app on my phone for my to-do list.
4. Use a notebook. The old fashion way. Use a spiral notebook or notepad.
5. Sticky notes. Sticky notes are nice because you can stick them anywhere so your goal/dream/deadline etc. is staring you in the face all the time. You can then post your notes on your monitor, the wall, your mirror in the bathroom, the fridge, by your bed, and just about anywhere else you will be looking frequently.
6. Use your smart phone's calendar. Today's technology has really revolutionized the way we do business. Using your smart phone's calendar can serve as an extremely beneficial tool for you on many levels. You can set reminders, repeats, enter goal dates several years in the future, add notes, and a multitude of other functions.
7. Use your email program's calendar. Your email program's calendar can be used in the same way as your smart phone's calendar. Another useful idea is to put client notes on the appointment entry for what you will or have discussed with each client. Before the client comes in for their appointment, you can open the appointment and prepare for your meeting.
8. Use a bulletin board. You can use a bulletin board to tack up your goal sheets, to-do lists, post-it notes, dream boards, etc. in a convenient and visible location.
9. White board. I used to write down import dates, notes, and projects in the corner of a white board in my room. You can also write motivational sayings on your whiteboard as a pick-me-up to look at during the day. A white board is an

easy to use, convenient, and visible way to put up very important information you need to keep front and center and can easily be erased when completed.
10. Tape/attach to a wall. If you don't have a bulletin board or its not in an easily viewable area, you can tape or sticky putty your notes close to you. (Be careful that it doesn't take the paint off the wall when you remove them!)
11. File your goals in a file cabinet. Use a file cabinet to file your goals in a folder. You can also use hanger files labeled by month so you can easily pull a file each month to see the projects you need to start or complete that month.
12. Put your goal sheets in a desk tray file organizer. There are many different types and looks for desktop file organizers. You can place your important (or all) of your goals in individual slots you can label by importance, date, due today (or week), or all together in one slot.
13. Lay your goal sheets in a pile on your desk. Desktop piles seem to be the method of choice for many people. If you are like me, extremely type "A" and organized, this won't work for you!

Managing Your Goals Recap

1. You should have short, mid, and long-term goals ranging from daily up to 20 years and retirement.
2. Write down your goal indicators so you know if you are on track to complete your goal and if you are meeting your completion standards.
3. Keep track of your goals in an easy to access location and source.

Week In Review Report

Another handy tool you can use to organize your week is called the "Week In Review Report," "Week At a Glance," or "Weekly Progress Report." The week in review report gives a snapshot glance of your past week's performance, issues, and what's ahead. Done properly, the week in review report will give you motivation from seeing what you got accomplished and get help for the things you didn't. This report (Figure 14) is filled out on the last day of the week (Friday if that is the end of your work week).

Week In Review Categories:

1. Week of: list the starting day of your week with day, month, and year. Or – you can list a range of dates from the first to the last day it covers.
2. Achievements this week: List 3 to 5 of the goals you accomplished this week. This is the first thing on your list and gives you a well deserved pat on the back.
3. Goals not accomplished and why: List the things you didn't get accomplished that you should have or wanted to get done. List the reasons why you didn't get them done. Listing the reasons will help you evaluate what you can do to get that goal done in the following week(s), avoid similar pitfalls in the future, or help you identify areas you need to solicit help.
4. Issues: List any problems you have faced during the past week so they can either become a future goal that needs to be addressed, avoided in the future, or solicit help.
5. Goals for next week: list your top 3 to 5 goals you really want or need to get accomplished next week. This is a high level overview and should be explained by the simple goal or project name. A goal sheet could accompany each goal or written out in your preferred method.

Week In Review Report

Week Of: _____

Achievements this week _____

_____

_____

_____

Goals not accomplished and why _____

_____

_____

_____

Issues _____

_____

_____

_____

Goals for next week _____

_____

_____

_____

Copyright 2014 Jason Gansen All Rights Reserved.

Figure 14

Week In Review Recap

1. A week in review report will help you to know where you are and where you are going each week at a glance.

Additional Resources & Links

1. Link to free download of the Week In Review:
    a. http://howtoevolveyourbusiness.com/

The Power of Visualization

Athletes, stunt pilots, and several other professionals use visualization as a technique to prepare themselves before an event. Visualization is when you imagine yourself performing exactly as you would in the real world.

Visualization helps you practice by going through all the motions in your mind.

Visualization for Goal Setting:

1. Find a comfortable, quiet place you can daydream and concentrate.
2. Think about all the reasons you have the goal.
3. Think about your objectives for your project and why you need or want to do it.
4. See in your mind's eye what your reward(s) is/are for achieving your objective. You can also create a dream board to help you visualize your reward (WIIFM).
5. See yourself starting with step one and continue until the goal has been completed within your mind.
6. Consider the obstacles you may encounter and watch yourself overcome these obstacles successfully.
7. Imagine what it will be like once your goal has been accomplished.
8. Use as many of your five senses as possible. What smells are in the air, what will you touch or feel, what will you see, what will you taste, and what will you hear?

I used the visualization technique to attain an award. It was getting toward the end of the goal period and I was nowhere near the numbers I needed to win.

I wrote my goal down and all the steps I needed to get there. There was a detailed, written plan I had to follow. I calmly sat down in a quiet area and daydreamed about the tasks before me.

It was a sales award, so I imagined myself calling my prospects and what I would say to them. I imagined myself entering the sales information into the computer system and the grin I would have on my face as I did it.

I thought about what I would do if people wouldn't meet with me or if they said "no" to the product I was selling and how I would react.

Then I began to think about the money I would receive and standing in front of my regional awards banquet holding onto my award as my manager presented it. It felt good… really good! I daydreamed about the possibilities I would have in my future because I earned the award. In my mind, my little adventure was a journey as real as I could imagine.

When I was finished, I felt refreshed and knew what I had to do for success. I had my goal well established and my motivation was at an all time high.

When I went to perform my action plan in the real world, I felt like I had already done it. I felt like I was on autopilot and only had to go through the motions.

I got back on track, but was only 1 sale away from success on the last sales day of the month. Out of nowhere, a walk-in client came to my office and I closed the deal. It was one of the greatest and most powerful experiences I've had.

The Power of Visualization Recap

1. Athletes, pilots, and many other professions utilize visualization often.
2. Visualizing your rewards and already accomplishing your goals before it happens will give you confidence, motivation, and help you practice before doing to complete your goals more efficiently.

Additional Resources & Links

1. Go to WikiHow and search for "How to visualize"

2. Go to your favorite search engine online and search for "How to use visualization to achieve your goals" for more information, pictures, and videos.

Quotes On Goals

- Temporary defeat is not permanent failure ~Napoleon Hill

- "Where there's a will, there's a way." ~Old English Proverb

- "Winners never quit and quitters never win." ~Vince Lombardi

- "It's not over until I win!" ~Les Brown

- "Plan your work and work your plan." ~Margaret Thatcher

- "A good plan today is better than the perfect plan tomorrow." (Indecision and Procrastination are killers.) ~Proverb and quote from the movie "The Edge" 1997.

- "Shoot for the moon. Even if you miss, you'll land among the stars." ~Les Brown (If you aim for a higher goal than you think you can achieve, you may not reach it, but your results will be higher than if you shoot for a lower, easier goal to attain.)

- "If you don't have a goal, you won't reach it." ~Variant of the quote from Yogi Berra, "If you don't know where you are going, you'll end up someplace else."

Final Thought on Goals

You may ask yourself "Why would I want to spend all this extra time and energy to write out, track, file, study, visualize, and everything else discussed here for my goals? It seems like extra work to go through all this trouble when I could skip goal setting and get started on my project."

Hopefully you've learned that by goal setting you will complete your goals more efficiently, better, and faster. The real question is, "Why would I want to take 2 to 10 times as long to complete a project or never complete it at all if I don't go through the goal setting process?"

Once I started setting daily goals again for writing this book, I was able to finish this section on goals in less than a month.

I've heard this quote many times throughout my life from many different sources. I don't know where this quote comes from, but I think it fits this final thought really well. I believe a version of this quote came from the movie Platoon in 1986.

"Excuses are like a$$holes. Everybody has one!"

Section 3: Decision Making

Figure 15

Luck Versus Decision Making

We make decisions every day. Some are simple, "Should I eat cereal or eggs for breakfast?" Some are complex, "Should I buy a house or rent?" Some are life altering, "Which major should I choose in college?" Some are straightforward, "Should I drink coffee today?" Of course I want coffee!

How do you know which decision is the right one? How do you know what consequences you'll face if you don't choose correctly? In business, making the wrong choice could cost you a client or cause you to lose your job or company.

How does luck effect your decisions? Choosing A or B has a 50/50 chance of getting the right one. I'm sure you have made a decision you pulled out of the air more than once. Sometimes you get lucky and sometimes you suffer the consequences.

Could it be that lucky people are channeling an inner mechanism? Could they have a conscious or subconscious decision making skill that makes them appear lucky? Could their minds be focusing on the presented facts, past experiences, education, and a little intuition? I think the latter is the true reality.

To improve your chances of picking the right choice is a matter of looking at the facts and considering the consequences. If you want to try your luck, pull the answer out of a hat and see what happens. If you want to increase your odds of being happy, make more money, and improve your life, then continue reading.

Some people are naturally gifted when it comes to decisions. I watch Shark Tank every Friday and noticed one of the gifts the super rich have – they have a gut feeling and usually go with it.

I am guessing wealthy people have learned what will produce a winner or a loser. They have learned through their upbringing, social interaction, friends, education, what has worked in the past, etc. Wealthy people pay attention to decision making clues.

I doubt the affluent and prosperous are winners because they are luckier than the rest of us. Remember what my dad always said, "The harder I work, the luckier I get?" You do have to work hard to get what you want out of life and climb the success ladder. On the other hand, my dad also told me, "Work smarter, not harder." Making the wrong decisions could create more work for you than you need to do.

In this section, I hope I can shed a little light on how you will make decisions by making educated choices rather than lucky guesses. With a little work and planning, you can increase your decision making skills.

Let's do an exercise to begin our decision making journey. Look at the picture at the beginning of this section (Figure 15). There are two frames - frame A and frame B. If your boss told you, "Pick one," which one would you choose?

Could you make a choice with the information you have? At this point, you are basing your decision solely on luck. You will need to ask some questions to get a better understanding why your boss wants the frame.

1. Is the frame for business or personal?
2. Did his wife tell him to get the frame and he delegated it to you? What kind of things does Mrs. Boss like? What is going in the frame and where will it be hung?
3. What décor is in the room this will go in?
4. Is the frame going to be a one-time purchase? Is it going to be an order for many frames or one? Can you buy them in bulk and from whom?
5. Are the frames going to be used for resale?
6. Who is the target customer if they are for resale?
7. What are the purchase prices, budget, and allowable markup?
8. Are the frames made from safe materials? Are they toxic? Are they sturdy? How long will they last? When will they start fading or deteriorate? Are the frames for outside or inside?
9. What have others thought of the frames after purchase?
10. What are the shipping costs? Can you pick them up? What stores carry them? Can you buy them from the

manufacturer? Can you have them made cheaper than buying them? Is there a patent on the frames?

Can you see where I'm going with this? If not, here are a few traits of decision making:

1. Decisions are based on facts.
2. Decisions could be based on opinions.
3. Decisions can be made on tangible or intangible things.
4. Decisions can have consequences or could be inconsequential.
5. Decisions could require additional information and necessitate further questioning.
6. Decisions require talking to the correct person.
7. Decisions may require additional resources like time, money, or help.
8. What is your gut feeling?
9. Have you ever made a decision like this before? What was the outcome? Should you make a different choice this time?

The point is there are questions that need to be answered before you can make any decision. You may have to ask many questions before you can go further. Sometimes asking one question could eliminate some or all of your further questions. Having a method for organizing your data and knowing which questions to ask will be tremendously helpful.

Don't rely on luck when you don't have to. Tip the scales in your favor. The following chapters will provide you with some details to consider as you move forward in life and career.

Luck vs Decision Making Recap

1. Successful people utilize a gut feeling and go with it or at least pay attention to it.
2. Your decision making gut feeling comes from: upbringing, social interactions, friends, education, past careers, past experiences.
3. Asking the correct questions will lead you toward the correct answer

The For/Against Method

The for/against method of decision making is a technique I've used since grade school. It is probably the easiest method that will give you an advantage when deciding which direction to take. This method is typically for binary decisions:

1. Yes/no
2. Do it/Don't do it
3. For/Against
4. This way or that way

Start by making two columns on a piece of paper. One column will be marked For, Advantages, or Positives and the other is Against, Disadvantages, or Negatives (Figure 16). Write down as many positives in the positives column and as many negatives as you can in its respective column.

There are two ways to decipher the chart to make a decision. The first way is to simply choose the column with the most items listed. If you have 10 positives and 4 negatives, then choose "for" the decision. If you have 7 positives and 8 negatives, then chose against.

The second way to analyze your chart is to evaluate the weight or importance of each column. For example, if you have 10 items in the Positives column and 1 item in the negative, you would choose to go with the positive column. What if the 1 negative item is any one of the following?

1. "I will end up getting divorced"
2. "I will end up in jail"
3. "I will lose my job"
4. "I could lose everything and become homeless"

Those are pretty severe negatives! If your decision is, "Should I punch my boss in the face because he is a jerk and he deserves it," you will definitely need to weigh all the consequences of your actions. The weight of the negative column has higher consequences than the positives no matter how good it would feel in the moment.

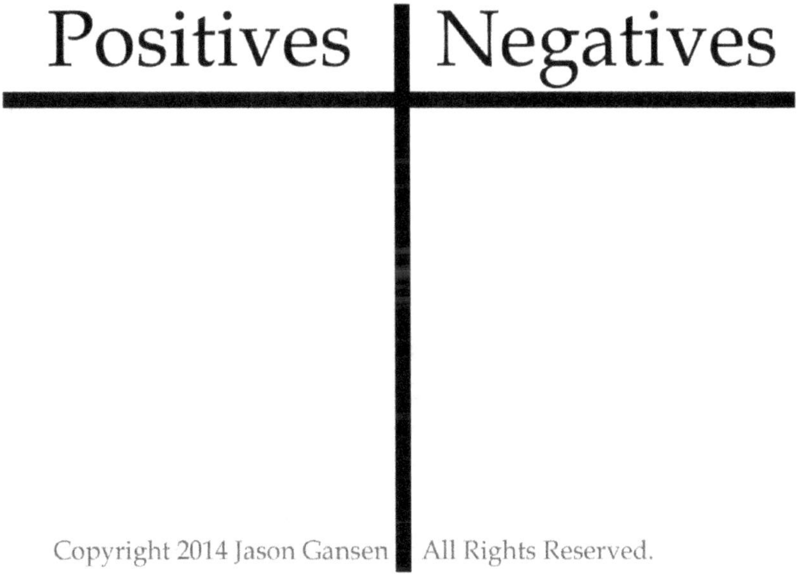

Positives	Negatives

Copyright 2014 Jason Gansen   All Rights Reserved.

Figure 16

One of the challenges kids or teens face when making decisions is thinking about the consequences in the future. Kids like to live in the here and now and don't think ahead. They want what they want and they want it now.

Your decision might seem like the proper choice right now. It may seem like the correct thing to do, but how will your decision affect you or others a month, a year, or 10 years down the road?

When making your for/against chart, factor in short term and long-term consequences as a positive or negative.

Here is an example of using the for/against chart for moving offices I used several years ago. I was trying to determine if moving would be a smart decision even though my manager didn't feel it was right for me (Figure 17). Try to figure out what my decision was as you read through the chart.

Advantages	Disadvantages
1. Less expensive than current	1. New office is difficult to find
2. Furniture supplied	2. My clients could become frustrated by trying to find my new office
3. Office equipment and supplies included	
	3. I will have to change my adds, business cards, letter head, etc.
4. Will share an office with someone experienced that can provide help and counseling	4. I will have to contact all clients and prospects to let them know new phone number and address.
5. Two full time staff included	
6. I will be more successful and make more money	5. Expense of moving
	6. Limited offer – I have to make a decision within 48 hours.

Figure 17

As you can see, the columns have the same number of items listed. This was a very conflicted decision. Did you guess what my final decision was? I looked closely at the weight of each item and the future consequences.

I concluded that even though it would be a lot of up front expense to move, the money I saved each month and additional income from working with an expert would well out weigh the initial consequences of going against my manager.

Another example is a for/against chart for a major life decision. Jamie S. is a friend of mine that started getting physically, mentally, and emotionally abused within a week or two of her wedding. What was supposed to be the happiest days of her life became a nightmare.

Jamie waited months in fear before she leaned on the support of her friends and family. The decision to leave her new husband was really scary for her in every way imaginable. Here is her chart (Figure 18) to help her decide whether she should leave or stay with him:

Positives For Leaving Him	Negatives for Leaving Him
1. Have a chance of being happy again	1. We own a business together – will lose my job
2. I've needed medical attention from him beating me	2. Will lose my home
3. I've lost a lot of friends because he won't let me talk to others like I used to and I could get my friends back	3. Will lose my new husband
	4. He told me I will lose friends
	5. Will lose my life as I know it - Job, home, being a wife
4. I am made to lie for him	6. I am his wife and should stand by his side
5. I have to cover for him	7. We just got married and things could get better
6. I might not be as lucky in the future	8. I won't have any money and a lot of debt racked up from business

Figure 18

As you can see, her negatives to leave her new husband was greater than the positives, but her physical safety and future happiness well outweighed staying with him.

The story does have a happy ending. Jamie was able to get a divorce and used her story on the local news to provide inspiration to others in similar situations.

Jamie enlisted the help of Break The Silence during her struggles of abuse and has since become an advocate and speaker for the group. She is now living a happy life and engaged to a great guy that treats her like she deserves.

If you want more information about Break The Silence for you or someone you know, go to "Break the Silence Against Domestic Violence" on Facebook or go to their website: http://www.breakthesilencedv.org/

Here are some prompts to get you going if you are having trouble thinking of items to put in your positives and negatives columns:

1. What financial effects will the decision have?
2. Will the decision affect any friendships/relationships/business ties?
3. What are the short-term consequences?
4. What are the long-term consequences?
5. Will further education be required?
6. Are the resources readily available? (Time, Money, Personnel)
7. Are there any ethical, moral, legal obligations that will sway my decision?
8. Have I ever come across a similar situation in the past? What would I change about that decision?
9. What is my gut feeling?
10. Are there any experts I can consult?
11. Are there any physical or mental constraints or consequences?
12. What other features, benefits or detriments should be included in the decision?
13. Will the decision affect another person, animal, environment, etc.? If so, how?
14. What are the underlying reasons for the decision?
15. If the decision being made came from someone else, are you getting all of the information needed? Are you talking to the ultimate decision maker?
16. Will this decision influence or change other decisions?

17. Will this decision have to be made again in the future?

The For/Against Method Recap

1. Using a For/Against chart will help your decisions become a little more black and white
2. Closely scrutinize the weight of each item in the positive and negative columns
3. How will the consequences of your decision affect you in the future?

Additional Resources & Links

1. www.breakthesilencedv.org

The Five Question Method

If the decisions you need to make are more complex than yes/no, right/wrong, true/false, then you will want to use the Five Question Method. I was originally introduced to this method about fifteen years ago and have revised it a few times. I have decided to list the three variants to allow you to choose which best suits your needs.

Method 1:

1. Organization
2. Gather facts and data
3. What is your gut feeling?
4. What are the negatives?
5. What are the positives or "Out of the Box" thinking?

Let's go back to my original scenario of the frames. Your boss has asked you to choose a frame from either A or B. Here is one way to make this decision using method 1 (See Figure 19).

Figure 19

1. My boss wants me to pick a frame. Further investigation revealed that my boss wants to purchase 100 of them for resale.
2. There are 25 museums that have contacted our company to purchase frames. The frames are to showcase replica paintings from famous artists. The canvases can be made to fit either frame.
3. Frame B will be able to fit horizontal and vertical pictures, so are more versatile. Frame B has a museum quality and look to them.
4. We don't sell frames and haven't sold them before. Frame A looks more majestic, but has more of a church look to it than a museum look. Frame A can only be hung vertically. Frame B has a higher demand and is back ordered for 2 months. Could have issues getting 100 of them.
5. Selling the frames will be very lucrative for our company and could lead to additional sales. Due to the back order, the manufacturer has agreed to let me find a different manufacturer for the first order until they get caught up if we pay them a 5% licensing fee.

Decision is to purchase frame B.

Method 2:

1. State the issue
2. What is my gut feeling and initial thinking?
3. List the negatives
4. List the positives
5. What is the solution?

6. What is needed to make the solution happen?
7. Evaluate and revise as needed.

Heidi is from Sunny Radio. To listen in Sioux Falls, SD their station is at 92.1 FM, Sioux City, IA at 1250 AM, or on the web at – http://www.mysunnyradio.com/ to listen live. Their Facebook page is Sunny Radio. Heidi helped me with a scenario she recently came across where she used method 2.

1. "I am leaving town for a few days and we are down to two vehicles because the business vehicle is getting the new stereo installed. John, my husband, needs a vehicle for work and our son needs to get himself and his sister to and from school.
2. I went onto Craigslist and thought about buying another vehicle. Maybe I can rent one?
3. The negatives are that this is definitely poor timing on my part. The business vehicle will be done Friday so I could wait until next week to make this trip- but I REALLY need to go. We do have a 13 passenger "bus" that Sunny Radio owns, so I guess that could work for somebody (John) but it is such a gas-guzzler and not practical at all.
4. I will be much happier when I return and when mommy's happy everybody's happy. :) The bus is a 3rd vehicle and will work since John spends most of his day at Sunny Radio and rarely drives around.
5. I am going! I get the van, and our son gets his car
6. The good news is we don't need anything additional - it was all here the whole time; I just never considered the bus as an option. When you step back and think - it all comes together."

Decision is to utilize one of our business vehicles

Method 3:

1. What is the true, underlying decision that needs to be made?
2. What data is available to make the decision?
3. After analyzing the facts, what is my initial thoughts and reaction?

4. What experts are available to help you make the decision? (This does not include family and friends if they are not experts unless the decision directly concerns them).
5. What are the positives and negatives?
6. What are the consequences of the decision?
7. Finalize the decision, implement, and revise as needed.

Teresa is a friend of my family and told me she has an issue with a couple trees that were attracting box elder bugs on her property. She had an issue deciding what to do with the trees, so I asked her to use method 3 to come up with a solution. Here is her thought process and resolution.

1. "I hate these 2 trees I have in my back yard. They are box elder trees and last summer I had a swarm of box elder bugs on my chimney. I called a guy last night whom is the only person I know of who does this type of thing in town. My underlying issue is finding a way to get rid of the box elder bugs on my property. (Revised issue – three trees need to be removed due to safety issues and to get rid of box elder bugs.)
2. I did a Google search to find his number. I asked him to give me a price on cutting one down versus cutting both of them down. He came over for an estimate and showed me how bad one of my trees was. I thought I had two trees, but he showed me there were actually three. He showed me how one tree is hollow and could fall down at any time.
3. Because of where they are located, the worst tree needed to be the last tree to come down. All three have to come down and will be a lot more expensive than originally planned. There really isn't a choice whether or not to take all three down now due to safety concerns.
4. The expert is the tree guy. Based on his analysis of the trees being dangerous, in addition to the box elder bug problem, they need to come down.
5. Positives for removing the trees – they attract bugs, one tree is badly damaged and could fall down on its own, and the trees are an eye sore so the property will look better once they are gone. Negatives for removing the trees – all three

have to be removed instead of only two and it will cost a lot more than I originally saved for.
6. If I don't remove them, the badly damaged tree could fall and hurt someone or damage property. The tree guy said he would buy my trailer that he noticed while looking at the trees. He could apply the price of the trailer to what I would owe. Selling the trailer would get the price closer to what I was originally anticipating and had saved.
7. I will sell him the trailer, get rid of all three trees, and get it done before our graduation reception for our daughter. Tree guy is scheduled to remove all three trees."

Decision is to cut down all three trees/ sell trailer to pay for it.

Here are some points to think about when you are using the multiple question method.

1. Always find the underlying issue. A clearly defined issue or decision to make will help you follow the correct path to resolution. In the example with Teresa, she thought the real issue was box elder bugs, but in it was in fact the rotten tree that had to be removed. If she had tried to spray for the bugs, the real issue would have still existed.
2. Always gather and analyze the facts. Investigate what needs to be done, consult experts, and do your research. Examine your data and take note of your initial gut feeling.
3. Always look at the positives and negatives for the decision you need to make. If needed, you can great a positive/negative, for/against chart.
4. Contemplate the consequences of your decision, the weighted value of the positives and negatives, the short and long-term effects, what has been done in the past, and whether or not the decision will need to be made again in the future. Ask yourself if there is an out-of-the-box solution that hasn't been used before for this situation.

5. Once you've decided on a final resolution, put together a plan, implement your plan, and evaluate your plan as you go to see if any revisions need to take place.

Pam Johnson has been in customer service for 58 years. Her parents owned a truck stop, she ran a deli and catering business at a grocery store, worked at a steak house, managed a Dairy Queen, and is currently a manager for a convenience store. Pam has an extensive background in customer service and management. As a result, she has had to refine and perfect her decision-making skills. Here are some of her tips on decision-making:

1. Remember to keep your mood in check when making decisions.
2. Think before you speak or act.
3. Sometimes it is better to keep your mouth shut.
4. Know all the facts before making a decision.
5. Don't include everyone in a class or group; don't come with preconceived ideas for someone, how they will act, or how they will respond.
6. Don't make hasty decisions.

The final segment of your decision making process is the effect your decision will have on others. Many years ago, I had a manager that taught her employees the Triangle of Success.

If you search the Internet on the Triangle of Success, you will find a lot of great stuff, but it is different from this version. I haven't been able to find any data on the origin of her adaptation of the Triangle of Success and haven't seen it used this way since. The results of her version are incredibly powerful.

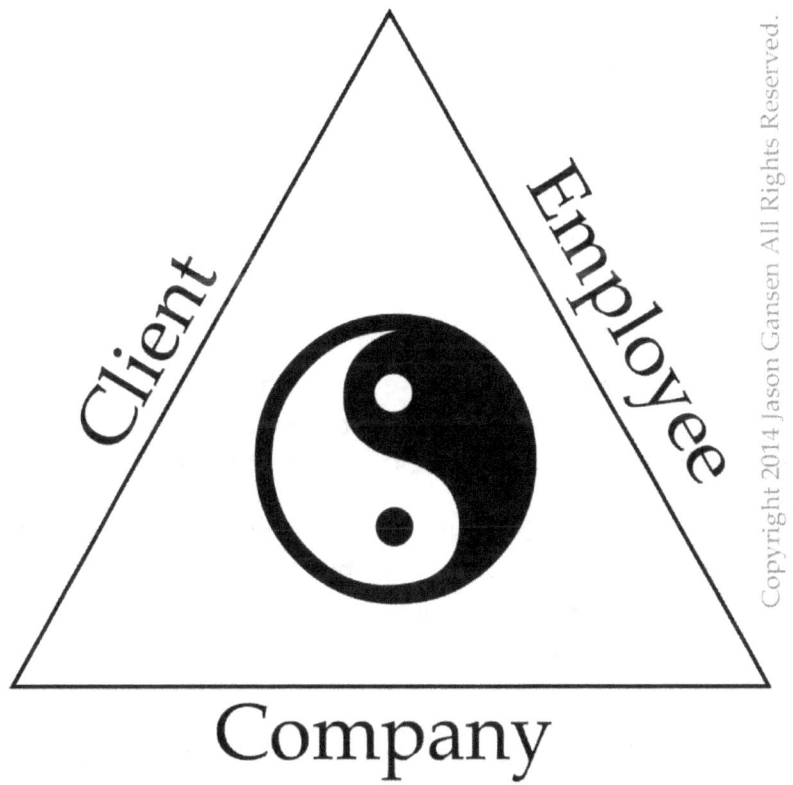

Figure 20

The Triangle of Success (Figure 20): Any time you make a decision, think about the consequences and effects your decision will have on the other two sides of the triangle. All three sides are intertwined and linked together. If one side has a negative end result, the other two sides will have a negative end result. The reverse is true for positive effects as well.

Let's say the company has decided to eliminate the Christmas bonus to cut back on expenses. The company thinks they can pass the savings on to the clients, which should drive more traffic and sales. This is a great idea and could possibly work; however, here is a scenario that is more likely to occur:

Since the bonus is eliminated, the employees become upset. The employees won't get to pay for the presents they had planned on, go on that trip they waited for all year, catch up on bills, etc. If you have ever seen the movie "Christmas Vacation" with Chevy Chase, you've seen this part in action.

The next thing that will happen is the company now has a bunch of disgruntled employees working for them. They won't be as productive, they may not treat the customers as they had in the past, and they lose motivation. Ultimately, the disgruntled employees could end up quitting or getting fired.

If the employees are unhappy, they will pass that sentiment on to the clients. The clients won't return if they had a bad purchasing, sales or delivery experience or poor customer service. Worst yet, the dissatisfied client could tell others about their experience.

The company suffers if the clients won't return, prospects won't buy, or others avoid the company because of the bad word being spread. If sales decrease, production needs to decrease or prices need to drop resulting in… you guessed it… another pay decrease for employees. The cycle continues.

On the flip side, if you make the employees happy, they treat the clients better because they love their job; happy clients become return purchasers - thus making a prosperous company.

Without equilibrium, the triangle will fail. With an equal triangle, all three sides can find happiness, success, and prosper. The evenly balanced Ying and Yang will help everyone involved get what they want.

The Five-Question Method Recap

1. For more complex questions or to help decipher the weight of each point in your decisions, use the 5 question method.
2. The Five Questions:
   a. Organization
   b. Gather Facts and data
   c. What is your gut feeling?
   d. What are the negatives?
   e. What are the positives or out-of-the-box thinking?
3. Always find the underlying issue when making decisions. Look past the symptoms or results of the issue and find what

is causing the symptoms to occur in the first place.
4. Think before you speak or act.
5. Know all the facts before making a decision.
6. Don't react too quickly when making your decisions.
7. Consider the triangle of success when making decisions. How will your decision affect:
    a. Your clients
    b. Your employees
    c. Your company

Additional Resources & Links

1. http://www.mysunnyradio.com

Creating Your Mastermind

Groups help like-minded individuals come together. They can enjoy talking about what they do or love and they can engage in activities that are mutually beneficial. Totally engulf yourself in information and knowledge. Joining a group or club will also help you engage in what you want to learn about or enjoy.

A group of individuals can also motivate each other. If you join a book club, you are motivated to read more so you don't return to the group with nothing to talk about. If you are in sales, you are more motivated to go out and sell so you don't come back empty handed. If you join a group that helps the community or church, the group will hold you accountable to do good things or help out with events or charities.

You can learn a lot from groups you become a member of. You can help the community and create a business network to help promote your business or sales. I co-founded a sales group a few years ago with a friend of mine. We had salesmen from different fields that met once every two weeks to discuss sales ideas. I learned some of my best and favorite sales techniques from this group while enjoying the company of the members. As a bonus, we had fun in the process!

Another thing you will find by creating or joining a group is a phenomenon called "The Mastermind." The insightful and inspiring book, "Think and Grow Rich" by Napoleon Hill discusses the "Power of the Mastermind" in Chapter 10. One of the concepts from this states that when two or more people come together with ideas, a third virtual mind is created. People that have their own ideas and thoughts, when brought together will come up with ideas the individual may not have thought of.

This is a great concept when you are trying to figure something out, learn something new, or enjoy your craft. Surround yourself with like-minded individuals that will motivate and teach you. To be successful, you will want to be around people that have achieved what you desire.

If you come across difficult decisions and the decision making techniques are not helping you to produce a desirable resolution, present your problem to your mastermind group. They could tell you whether or not you are on the correct path, or provide you with another direction.

Find a group or start one, benefit yourself from the knowledge you can learn from a group, become more successful with the things you desire, and most importantly - have fun.

Quotes On Decision Making

From:
http://www.brainyquote.com/quotes/keywords/decision-making.html - UCFXdcrighgdaGkA.99

- If a decision making process is flawed and dysfunctional, decisions will go awry. ~Carly Fiorina

- Inability to make decisions is one of the principal reasons executives fail. Deficiency in decision making ranks much higher than lack of specific knowledge or technical know-how as an indicator of leadership failure. ~John C. Maxwell

From: http://www.slideshare.net/powersayings/10-decision-making-quotes

- Stay Committed to your decisions, but stay flexible in your approach. ~Tom Robbins

- Indecision becomes decision with time. ~Author Unknown

- When a decision has to be made, make it. There is no totally right time for anything. ~General George Patton

- Where this is no decision there is no life. ~Author Unknown

- If you chase two rabbits, both will esccape. ~Author Unknown

From: http://www.quotegarden.com/decisions.html

- It's not hard to make decisions when you know what your values are. ~Roy Disney

- When one bases his life on principle, 99 percent of his decisions are already made. ~Author Unknown

- The hardest thing to learn in life is which bridge to cross and which to burn. ~David Russell

- Good decisions come from experience, and experience comes from bad decisions. ~Author Unknown

- Once you make a decision, the universe conspires to make it happen. ~Ralph Waldo Emerson

From: http://www.decision-making-confidence.com/decision-quotes.html

- "The roads we take are more important than the goals we announce. <u>Decisions determine destiny</u>." ~Frederick Speakman

- "A wise man makes his own decisions, an ignorant man follows public opinion." ~Chinese proverb

- "When people are free to do as they please, they usually imitate each other." ~Eric Hoffer

- "Indecision and delays are the parents of failure." ~George Canning

- "It's much better to prepare and not have the opportunity than to have the opportunity and not be prepared." ~Anon

- "In a moment of decision, the best thing you can do is the right thing to do. The worst thing you can do is nothing." ~Theodore Roosevelt

- "When making a decision of minor importance, I have always found it advantageous to consider all the pros and cons. In vital matters, however, such as the choice of a mate or a profession, the decision should come from the unconscious, from somewhere within ourselves. In the important decisions of personal life, we should be governed, I think, by the deep inner needs of our nature." ~Sigmund Freud

Creating Your Mastermind Recap

1. Joining a group or club will help motivate you and increase your knowledge. It will also contribute to your life balance.
2. Being part of a mastermind group will increase your knowledge and help to create ideas the individuals of the group may not have come up with otherwise.
3. If you can't find the right group for you – make one.

Tying It All Together

The beginning of all business and personal ventures begins with motivation, continues with the proper planning, and always leads you toward frequent decisions. This book has given you a pathway toward success.

1. We can create our own luck in business and in life.
2. All things begin with motivation. Whether you are deciding to get out of bed in the morning or selling your start up company for $5 million dollars, you need to find what drives you. Look deep within yourself to find why you do what you do.
3. Once you find out why you are moving forward, backward, or side-to-side, your well thought out plan will propel you to success. Use S.M.A.R.T. goals, write them down, and set your deadlines. Learn from and follow the successful people that are where you want to be.
4. Using an analytical approach to decision making will help reduce risk and regret. Get expert advice to help you make decisions when you are not the expert. Always think about the consequences of your decisions.

In my opinion, one of the best stories on motivation, decision making, believing in yourself, and knowing your destination is the Rocky Story. Anything is possible through belief. The Rocky Story as told by Anthony Robbins is the success story of Sylvester Stallone. Sly came from very humble beginnings, but always knew his outcome and followed his dream to be an actor. The only way to do the story justice, other than hearing it from Stallone himself, is to hear it from Tony Robbins. I don't want to get into the meat of the story, because I can't do it justice.

Give yourself one of the biggest gifts possible for the success of your career and listen to this 9 minute and 20 second video.

1. Go to Youtube and search for: "Tony Robbins tells Rocky Story (The Original)"
    a. The best one I've found is the one with over 742,000 views.
2. Click on the following link:
    b. https://www.youtube.com/watch?v=ywuse55qU2A

We've covered a lot so far during the beginning of this journey together. I'm in it for the long haul if you are. I want to continue giving you the information I've learned and taught for the past 20 years, so watch for the next two books in this series, "How To Evolve Your Business With Sales, Marketing, and Customer Services."

Book two in this series is on the dos and don'ts of business, sales, and marketing.

Book three in this series is on closing the sale, referrals, and the extras.

Watch for these two books that will complete this series, their progress, and when they will be available on http://www.amazon.com/author/jasongansen, my website: http://jasongansen.webs.com/ and my blog: http://authorjasongansen.blogspot.com/ Follow me on Facebook at: "Author Jason Gansen" and "How to Evolve Your Business" and Twitter at: @locallybuilt.

Make sure to sign up with your email address so I can send you updates, additional business information, and pictures. One thing I hate is getting emails several times a day or even every couple of days from companies I have given my email address to. Rest assured, I will limit my emails to important, worthwhile information.

Go to http://howtoevolveyourbusiness.com/ to get your free download of the worksheets that are in this book. I truly feel this free download will help you tie all the information together that you've learned in this book and will help you continue toward your success.

By entering your email address, you will be put on my mailing list. Your information will never be sold and will be kept confidential. I respect your privacy. I only want success and good things to come your way.

These books will eventually be made available as an audio book and a full training course. I will do my best to get you the details as soon as they become available if you follow me on any of my sources listed above from the Internet and my email subscription.

Do Your Due Diligence

I have tried to make this book as complete and accurate as possible. This list of facts, opinions, deductions, and knowledge is a great start, but not a complete list of items to follow.

I have tried to find the original sources of all the information and quotes I've learned over the years from managers, others in the business world, and even from my own trials and errors. If I have misrepresented or listed in error credit for any information, I sincerely apologize, it was unintentional. I will gladly add any verified credit in my works cited.

The experts I interviewed and my own knowledge is limited to our experiences and beliefs. It is up to you to verify any of the knowledge here and to complete your own investigation. I am not and cannot be responsible for your successes or failures. It is impossible to know everyone's specific situation, but I feel confident that this guide will get you going in the right direction.

This book has been written to help anyone on a personal or professional level in sales or in business. Keep that in mind while implementing your specific plan from this book. Do your own investigation and soul searching to figure out what is holding you back on the journey toward your success.

Download a digital copy of this book on Amazon.com for $.99 if you've purchased the paperback from Amazon.com

About The Author – Jason Gansen

A jack-of-all-trades, Jason has been a professional pilot, teacher, motivational speaker, mentor, author, and coach for the past twenty-plus years in one form or another. His typical genre is nonfiction with how to, self-help, instructional, and his personal aviation stories from his career as a pilot.

"How To Evolve Your Business With Sales, Marketing, and Customer Service – Motivation, Goals, and Decision Making" is his first book in a three book series to help improve your business, sales, and life. If you are interested in learning more about Jason Gansen, or to get more information for the release dates of book 2 and 3 in this series, go to:

His blog to learn business, sales, and self help tips: authorjasongansen.blogspot.com
His website to learn more about the author, appearance dates and schedule, and to keep up to date on current/future projects, and look for free downloads: http://jasongansen.webs.com

To purchase more of Jason Gansen's books or to write a review:
http://amazon.com/author/jasongansen

Facebook:

"Author Jason Gansen"
"The Aviation Stories My Mom Didn't Want To Hear And I Lived To Tell"
"How to Evolve Your Business"

Twitter: @locallybuilt

THANK YOU

I personally wanted to say "thank you" for purchasing my book. There are a lot of options out there, so I really appreciate the time you took to read this.

If you enjoyed what you've learned here, then I need your help!

Please take a moment to leave an unbiased review for this book on Amazon:

http://www.amazon.com/author/jasongansen

This feedback lets me know if my book was liked and gives you a chance to provide information directly to potential readers and me. If there were things you enjoyed in the book, or things that might need some work, this is your opportunity to help out.

Thank you in advance for the review, and thanks again for choosing my book!

Sincerely,

Works Cited

"10 Decision Making Quotes to Improve Your Decision Making Skills." 10 Decision Making Quotes to Improve Your Decision Making Skills. SlideShare, n.d. Web. 1 May 2014. <http://www.slideshare.net/powersayings/10-decision-making-quotes>.

"Anonymous Insurance Agent." Personal interview. 24 Oct. 2013.

"Charles R. Swindoll Quotes." Thinkexist.com. ThinkExist, n.d. Web. 04 Apr. 2014. <http://thinkexist.com/quotes/charles_r._swindoll/>.

"Dealing with Poor Performance: Is It Lack of Ability or Low Motivation?" Dealing with Poor Performance. Mind Tools, n.d. Web. 01 May 2014. <http://www.mindtools.com/pages/article/newTMM_80.htm>.

"Decision Making Quotes." BrainyQuote. Xplore, n.d. Web. 1 May 2014. <http://www.brainyquote.com/quotes/keywords/decision-making.html#UCFXdcrighgdaGkA.99>.

"Denny Erickson." Telephone interview. 21 Oct. 2013.

"Dr. Tom Wullstein, PharmD." Personal interview. 8 Nov. 2013.

"Famous Quotes - Over 2.5 Million Funny, Inspirational, Life Quotes!" Famous Quotes - Over 2.5 Million Funny, Inspirational, Life Quotes! N.p., n.d. Web. 01 May 2014. <http://www.great-quotes.com/>.

"Free Personality Test." 16 Personality Types. MentiScore Solutions Limited, n.d. Web. 01 Nov. 2013. <http://www.16personalities.com/free-personality-test>.

"Heidi from Sunny Radio." E-mail interview. 18 Apr. 2014.

"How to Make a Dream Board." WikiHow: How to Make a Dream Board. WikiHow, n.d. Web. 03 Mar. 2014. <http://www.wikihow.com/Make-a-Dream-Board>.

"How to Save Thousands: Do It Yourself!" Amazon.com, 09 Sept. 2012. Web. <http://amzn.to/1lFthLq>.

"Jamie S." E-mail interview. 18 Apr. 2014.

"Pam Johnson." Personal interview. 4 Nov. 2013.

"Paranoia." IMDb. IMDb.com, n.d. Web. 01 May 2014. <http://www.imdb.com/title/tt1413495/?ref_=ttco_co_tt>.

"Personal Goal Setting: Planning to Live Your Life Your Way." Personal Goal Setting. Mind Tools, n.d. Web. 15 Dec. 2013. <http://www.mindtools.com/page6.html>.

"Quotes about Decisions (Decision Making, Choices, Deciding, Etc)." Quotes about Decisions (Decision Making, Choices, Deciding, Etc). The Quote Garden, n.d. Web. 01 May 2014. <http://www.quotegarden.com/decisions.html>.

"Rhonda Byrne." Amazon.com: : Books, Biography, Blog, Audiobooks, Kindle. N.p., n.d. Web. <http://www.amazon.com/Rhonda-Byrne/e/B001ILM8OQ/ref%3Dla_B001ILM8OQ_pg_2?rh=n%3A283155%2Cp_82%3AB001ILM8OQ&page=2&ie=UTF8&qid=1398997812>.

"Ryan Thomas." E-mail interview. 4 Nov. 2013.

"Teresa." E-mail interview. 18 Apr. 2014.

"The Top 10 Employee Motivators – and Demotivators." Lehigh Valley Business. Journal Multimedia, 15 July 2013. Web. 29 Apr. 2014. <http://www.lvb.com/article/20130715/LVB01/307119989/The-top-10-employee-motivators-%25E2%2580%2593-and-demotivators>.

"Tim Morris." E-mail interview. 4 Nov. 2013.

"Todd Ellingson." Personal interview. 24 Oct. 2013.

"Some peeps need to be reminded. The problem is not the problem. The problem is your attitude about the problem. Ultimately, you have complete control over whether you are happy or unhappy in life."

"Jason Yoshino, Energy Event Group." E-mail interview. 1 May 2014.

ApPro Services. "Free Aptitude Tests Online - Aptitude-Test.com." Free Aptitude Tests Online - Aptitude-Test.com. N.p., n.d. Web. 01 Nov. 2014. <http://www.aptitude-test.com/>.

Berra, Yogi. "A Quote by Yogi Berra." Goodreads. N.p., n.d. Web. 05 Apr. 2014. <http://www.goodreads.com/quotes/23616-if-you-don-t-know-where-you-are-going-you-ll-end>.

Blue Angels Power on the Prairie, Sioux Falls, SD. Personal photograph by author. 2012.

Brown, Les. "Les Brown Quotes." Les Brown Quotes (Author of Live Your Dreams). N.p., n.d. Web. 22 Apr. 2014. <https://www.goodreads.com/author/quotes/57803.Les_Brown>.

Brown, Les. "Quotegreetings." Quotegreetings. N.p., n.d. Web. 22 Apr. 2014. <http://quotegreetings.com/2013/its-not-over-until-you-win-les-brown/>.

Byrne, Rhonda. "Official Web Site of The Secret." Official Web Site of The Secret. N.p., n.d. Web. 01 May 2014. <http://thesecret.tv/>.

Churchill, Winston. "He, Who Fails to Plan, Plans to Fail." Search Quotes. N.p., n.d. Web. 05 Apr. 2014. <http://www.searchquotes.com/quotation/He%2C_who_fails_to_plan%2C_plans_to_fail./447242/>.

Cox, Coleman. Listen to This. San Francisco, CA: C. Cox Pub., 1922. Web.

D, J. "13 Negative Motivation Patterns." Sources of Insight. N.p., 2 Sept. 2007. Web. 01 Dec. 2013. <http://sourcesofinsight.com/13-negative-motivation-patterns/>.

David The Doctor From Dublin. "Decision Quotes for a Variety of Occasions." Decision-making-confidence.com. N.p., n.d. Web. 01 May 2014. <http://www.decision-making-confidence.com/decision-quotes.html>.

Doyle, Alison. "Best Answers for Top 50 Job Interview Questions." About.com Job Searching. Job Searching, n.d. Web. 01 Nov. 2013. <http://jobsearch.about.com/od/interviewquestionsanswers/a/top-50-job-interview-questions.htm>.

Ford, Henry. "A Quote by Henry Ford." Goodreads. N.p., n.d. Web. 06 Apr. 2014. <http://www.goodreads.com/quotes/978-

whether-you-think-you-can-or-you-think-you-can-t--you-re>.

Ford, Henry. "Henry Ford Quote." BrainyQuote. Xplore, n.d. Web. 07 Apr. 2014. <http://www.brainyquote.com/quotes/quotes/h/henryford101486.html>.

Foskett, Allison. "Step 5: Negative Motivation." Step 5: Negative Motivation. Peak Performance For Rising Women, n.d. Web. 01 Dec. 2013. <http://www.goal-setting-motivation.com/set-your-goals/negative-motivation/>.

Frazier, Matt. "5 'Easy' Steps for Making Your Unrealistic Goal a Reality." No Meat Athlete. N.p., 18 Nov. 2013. Web. 22 Dec. 2013. <http://www.nomeatathlete.com/big-goals-easy-steps/>.

Frost, David. "A Quote by David Frost." Quote by David Frost. Goodreads, n.d. Web. 13 Sept. 2013. <http://www.goodreads.com/quotes/171417-don-t-aim-for-success-if-you-want-it-just-do>.

Gambone, Gregory. "How to Use Negative Motivation in the Workplace." Small Business. Demand Media, n.d. Web. 01 Dec. 2013. <http://smallbusiness.chron.com/use-negative-motivation-workplace-16692.html>.

Glassman, Ifat. "Psychology of Selfishness: Positive vs. Negative Motivation." Psychology of Selfishness: Positive vs. Negative Motivation. Psychology of Selfishness, 11 Feb. 2009. Web. 01 Dec. 2014. <http://ifat-glassman.blogspot.com/2009/02/positive-vs-negative-motivation.html>.

Gray, Albert EN. The Common Denominator Of Success. Washington D.C.: National Association of Life Underwriters, 1992. Reprint.

Hill, Napoleon. "A Quote by Napoleon Hill." Goodreads. N.p., n.d. Web. 5 Apr. 2014. <http://www.goodreads.com/quotes/244859-a-dream-is-a-goal-with-a-deadline>.

Hill, Napoleon. Think and Grow Rich. New York: Fawcett, 1960. Print.

Kimbro, Dennis Paul, Napoleon Hill, and Napoleon Hill. Think and Grow Rich: A Black Choice. New York: Fawcett Columbine, 1991. Print.

Lee, Joel. "5 Critical Mistakes To Avoid When Setting Goals." 5 Critical Mistakes To Avoid When Setting Goals. MakeUseOf, 17 Jan. 2012. Web. 15 Dec. 2013. <http://www.makeuseof.com/tag/5-critical-mistakes-avoid-setting-goals/>.

Lombardi, Vince. "Vince Lombardi Quote." BrainyQuote. Xplore, n.d. Web. 22 Apr. 2014. <http://www.brainyquote.com/quotes/quotes/v/vincelomba122285.html>.

Mark Burnett Productions, prod. "Shark Tank." Shark Tank. ABC. N.d. Television.

Michener, H. A., J. A. Fleishman, and J. J. Vaske. "Journal of Personality and Social Psychology." Journal of Personality and Social Psychology (1976): 1114-126. Web. 9 Dec. 2004. A test of the bargaining theory of coalition formulation in four-person groups.

National Lampoon's Christmas Vacation. Dir. Jeremiah S. Chechik. By John Hughes. Perf. Chevy Chase, Beverly D'Angelo, Juliette Lewis. Warner Bros, 1989. DVD.

Old English Proverb. "English Proverbs." The Meanings and Origins of Sayings and Phrases. N.p., n.d. Web. 22 Apr. 2014. <http://www.phrases.org.uk/meanings/proverbs.html>.

Paranoia. By Joseph Finder. Screenplay by Barry L. Levy and Jason Hall. Dir. Robert Luketic. Perf. Liam Hemsworth, Gary Oldman, and Harrison Ford. Reliance Entertainment and Demarest Films, 2013. DVD.

Platoon. By Oliver Stone. Dir. Oliver Stone. Perf. Charlie Sheen, Tom Berenger, Willem Dafoe. MGM, 1986. DVD.

Radwan, M.Farouk. "The Ultimate Source for Understanding Yourself and Others." Positive and Negative Motivation. 2KnowMySelf.com, n.d. Web. 01 Dec. 2013. <http://www.2knowmyself.com/motivation/positive_negative_motivation>.

Sunny Radio, Sioux Falls, SD, n.d. Radio. http://www.mysunnyradio.com.

Swindoll, Charles R. "Charles R. Swindoll Quotes." Charles R. Swindoll Quotes (Author of The Grace Awakening). Good Reads, n.d. Web. 04 Apr. 2014. <https://www.goodreads.com/author/quotes/5139.Charles_R_Swindoll>.

Thatcher, Margaret. "Margaret Thatcher Quote." BrainyQuote. Xplore, n.d. Web. 22 Apr. 2014. <http://www.brainyquote.com/quotes/quotes/m/margaretth382871.html>.

The Edge. Dir. Lee Tamahori. By David Mamet. Perf. Anthony Hopkins, Alec Baldwin, Elle Macpherson. Fox, 1997. DVD.

Tony Robbins Tells Rocky Story (The Original). Perf. Tony Robbins, Sylvester Stallone. YouTube. N.p., 13 Feb. 2007. Web. 07 Apr. 20010. <https://www.youtube.com/watch?v=ywuse55qU2A>.

Wadud, Eric. "Section 5. Building and Sustaining Commitment." Community Toolbox. Work Group for Community Health and Development at the University of Kansas, 2013. Web. 29 Apr. 2014. <http://ctb.ku.edu/en/table-of-contents/leadership/leadership-functions/build-sustain-commitment/main>.

Whetten, David A., and Kim S. Cameron. Developing Management Skills. 6th ed. Glenview, Ill.: Prentice Hall, 2004. 299-300. Print.

Developing Management Skills. Amazon.com, n.d. Web. 01 May 2014. <http://www.amazon.com/Developing-Management-Skills-David-Whetten/dp/0131441426>.

Additional Titles By Jason Gansen

Available at http://www.amazon.com/author/jasongansen

A "how to" guide for saving or making money. Learn how to do many of the services, maintenance, construction projects, and troubleshooting you would normally pay someone else for and save money or start a business from a project you learned.

Sometimes the reasons we fall in love with someone are the same things that drive us apart. Prince Fletcher and Princess Callibella discover when love fades, time heals. As their relationship grows, they learn to love each other for different, stronger reasons. Their love develops into a power that is capable of conquering unbeatable odds.

Are you ready to take to the skies? As you plan your family's vacation make sure to include this book in your suitcase. My Airplane Ride - Scrapbook, Learning & Log provides children ages 3-10 a chance to document their trip with photos and information. Kids can pass the time on their journey learning the basics of flight. Is your child nervous about flying? This book provides vocabulary building opportunities, as well as simple answers and explanations about what they will hear, see, and feel on the plane.

Hang on to your seats! Action packed true-life stories from a perspective no one ever hears about. This is what happens in the air outside of the general public's eyes. From a student pilot to flying professionally, the title says it all! Now boarding: Humor, Action, Adventure, Fear and Adrenaline. Grab your sick-sack!

Jason Gansen has had a pilot license for 21 years. For the last 16 years, Jason has been writing down stories from friends and his own experiences from what it's like building an aviation career. After several close calls and ultimately losing his aviation medical, the stories are ready for the world, but is the world ready for them? Contains some strong language. Not suitable for young readers.

Each story is broken down into individualized, easy to read "chapters" in chronological order.

www.ingramcontent.com/pod-product-compliance
Lightning Source LLC
Chambersburg PA
CBHW081725170526
45167CB00009B/3702